TAPPING POTENTIAL

Achieving What You Want
with the
Abilities You Already Have

Kenneth J. Lodi

■

What Lies Behind Us and
What Lies Before Us
Are Tiny Matters Compared to
What Lies Within Us.

OLIVER WENDELL HOLMES

For those with questions, comments,
or wishing additional copies
of this book please call:

1-800-YOU-TAPP
(1-800-968-8277)

ISBN: 0-9646523-0-7

Book design and production by Robert S. Tinnon Design
Jacket design by Hespenheide Design

Printed and bound in the United States of America.

10 9 8 7 6 5 4 3

TO MY FAMILY
who has been so supportive over the years
in helping me tap my potential and
continue to make the journey possible.

CONTENTS

ACKNOWLEDGMENTS

I will never look at a book in the same way again. I love to read and tackle almost a book a week, and the experience of writing a book will forever make me appreciate the amount of work that so many people must contribute to make a book a *good* book. I wish to thank those people on this project who have provided encouragement, advice, and help in bringing this book to fruition.

First, I must thank my family for their support and patience, and for listening to me think aloud at dinners, ask for advice, and for acting as advisors. My father has always demonstrated that hard work pays off, and this completed project proves that the work ethic is true for everyone. My mother has always demonstrated that a special balance between intellect and instinct are good company on any journey; toss in a little love for what you do and you have a formidable recipe for success. She provided lots of encouragement when I needed it.

My brother has been a help twice on this project (I fired him once). His ideas were so intelligent, and he made it look so easy, I feared having a genius on my staff would threaten some of the others; after about an hour without him, I realized how much help he actually was, and so he was rehired. I never thought my kid brother's humanities degree from Yale would help *me* in so many ways. Thanks, Kevin.

A special thanks to Franklin Quest. Almost ten years ago I joined what was then a small company with a lot of promise. The founders, Hyrum Smith and Dick Winwood, felt that I had promise and gave me the opportunity to work with them in teaching principles of individual and organizational productivity. It has been truly rewarding to grow with these fine people and with an organization that is now a world leader in the industry.

I should also thank the thousands of people I have met in seminars who made contributions to discussions and allowed me to learn a great deal from them. They provided the necessary medium through which I could "test my material" and develop professionally.

I must thank Bob Tinnon and Rena Copperman for their advice and guidance in publishing this book. Without their patience and willingness to meet before work, after work, and on the weekends, it would have been a much rougher road.

Many people were sounding boards for me. I spent hours on the phone with two very good friends of mine, Rob Martwick and Dan Kotin. I want to thank Rob for his willingness to receive my calls during his busy schedule, his patience to read through the manuscript one page at a time to make constructive suggestions, and for his years of friendship; Dan and I have always helped each other "think things through," and I want to thank him for his helpful insights and for sharing in my enthusiasm for all of my pursuits over the years.

INTRODUCTION

> The best reformers the world has ever seen are those who
> begin on themselves.
>
> George Bernard Shaw

Have you ever asked yourself what it is about some people that makes them so successful? Have you ever admired these people and said, "I wish I could attain that level of success," or "I know I have the ability to be more successful, but I just don't know how to get there? What do they know that I don't know? What is their recipe for success that has enabled them to rise above the crowd?"

They have done what you possess the power to do for yourself. *They have learned how to tap their potential.* Essentially, we are no different from any of these high achievers. We can all think and make decisions; we all have natural talents, abilities, and other mental resources. We all know you must go the extra mile to get what you want. Some argue that top athletes or entrepreneurs have exceptional gifts. Perhaps some do, but most winners are people with *ordinary* talents who know how to apply them in *extraordinary* ways. It's not the ingredients, but how they are combined. The successes of this world have simply followed the right recipe. After all, three-time Olympic gold medalist Wilma Rudolph was born with a crippling polio condition, and the multi-billion-dollar film industry was built by a handful of immigrants who came to this country with absolutely nothing. Outstanding ingredients? Hardly. These people serve as great role models for the rest of the world as they demonstrate what can be achieved with the proper actions and attitudes. We can be these people.

We sometimes find ourselves stuck in a rut of mediocrity, and we stagnate not because of *who* we are (our potential), but because of *how* we are (our behavior). We will focus on how we can change behaviors to tap our potential and achieve success.

Our Objective

Potential is defined as "capable of being, but not yet in existence." Tapping potential involves finding the qualities in us that are "capable of being" *and bringing them into existence*. The principles in this book will allow you to make that leap from the potential to the actual so we can go from where we are to where we would like to be.

It's like the story of the man who had millions of dollars worth of oil reserves in his backyard. He was unaware of this until a prospector knocked on his door and told him of the distinct possibility that he may be sitting on great amounts of wealth and earnings potential for the rest of his life.

After some work, they discovered that the prospector was right. The owner of the house and the prospector for his advice and counsel became millionaires many times over. The key point is that the man who lived in the house *had been a millionaire all along*! His wealth was simply sitting there "untapped" until someone came along and helped him find it and bring it into his life.

You have vast reserves of the same kind of riches within reach. I am here to act as your prospector to help you tap those riches.

If you haven't been experiencing all you want in life, this book offers philosophies and strategies to help you reach your objectives. You already have the skills needed to be successful; here you will learn practical, effective methods that will help you put these skills to work.

Tapping Potential is not a single solution to all of life's challenges. There are no scientific breakthroughs here; it cannot do the work for you. What you will find in this book are effective strategies for tapping your personal potential, methods that will put you in control of your responsibilities, your goals, and your life.

After teaching thousands of individuals from corporate executives to self employed individuals in business, sports, and the arts, I have discovered that there are attitudes and practices shared by all winning personalities that separate them from those that *could be winners*. In the following chapters I will share these elements of successful living with the objective to guide and motivate you to apply yourself and realize your full potential.

It is human to put things off,
It is divine to start things off

W.H. DANFORTH

Let's start things off.

INDIVIDUALITY

I shall be telling this with a sigh
Somewhere ages and ages hence:
Two roads diverged in a wood, and I—
I took the one less traveled by,
And that has made all the difference.

ROBERT FROST

I have met a lot of people who are not happy with either their circumstances or performance. They believe their lives and careers have room for improvement if only they could do things differently. They feel as if they have fallen into a frustrating rut. They want their lives to be more stimulating, more exciting, and more adventurous.

Choosing Your Own Road

In order to make such a change you must create an individualized plan. To improve your chances of getting better results or climbing out of that rut, you can model yourself after successful people—adopting some habits of those who have succeeded and making those habits part of your routine. One common denominator I have observed in successful people is that they incorporate productive habits observed in the behavior of role models in their lives.

But they don't blindly do as others do. Successful people know that there is no such thing as a "one-size-fits-all" plan for achievement. Successful people create a personal plan that is tailored to their needs, one that differs from that of others. They confidently pursue a "road less traveled."

We all have the potential to improve performance and circumstances. To do this, we need to know how to tap our potential and avoid the trap of making the average performance our standard of performance. In other words, you must develop our own performance standards, and not follow the "average" way of doing things.

While many people are comfortable being a member of the "average" group, there is no glory in being like everybody else. Maintaining the status quo will never compare to the gratification of developing personally, achieving goals, and actively adding value to your life. You overlook much of your potential if you just go along with the crowd.

In order to tap your potential, you should consider living your life by standards, beliefs, and practices that are your own, not those of "most people."

You May Become Like Your Environment

College students sometimes refer to their college experience as a "five-year plan." Many claim that it is normal to change majors as often as three times, costing them an extra year in school. When learning that five years is normal and acceptable on campus, the student may consciously or subconsciously create a plan of accomplishing the four-year education in five years. The campus expectation has become self-fulfilling for many students.

A few years ago I made a presentation to a major computer manufacturing firm. I was to meet with a committee to customize a presentation we had planned for later that month. Although the meeting was scheduled for 8 A.M., only three of the expected eight people were present. At 8:15, I asked if we should get started and was surprised by their casual response.

"No, let's wait. They'll get here eventually. Meetings here never start on time. Would you like some coffee?"

Since nobody appeared to be under any great stress at the meeting starting late, I responded with, "Cream, no sugar." But what I was observing was far more significant than it appeared.

If people join the company and learn that "meetings never start on time," then feelings of apathy develop about ever being on time. The cycle continues, and it perpetuates the tradition of never trying to be punctual. It eventually results in a trend of poor productivity and costly meetings.

What is needed is a change in beliefs and standards. There should never be a question about what time the eight o'clock meeting starts.

There are many examples in life where we justify our behavior by what others do. We assume that if it is human, normal, or the standard, how bad could it be? It may not be harmful per se, but it can be an inhibitive factor in tapping our potential. And since most people have not tapped their potential, we must be careful not to measure our successes against those of others.

How to Shoot Yourself in the Foot

I recall a specific case where the XYZ company was to deliver a product presentation to some potential distributors. The distributors agreed to make a visit to the XYZ company, and they arrived about fifteen minutes early.

The XYZ people drifted in between ten and twenty minutes late and proceeded to "track down" an overhead projector and VCR. This last minute scramble didn't come across as a real professional effort. XYZ's punctuality skills had not been put into practice in some time and now it was going to cost them.

They made a bad impression; no contract was signed, and the entire poor performance was self-inflicted and preventable.

If your desire is to be one of the crowd, then just follow the crowd. If you would like to do better than the crowd, study top-performing individuals and adopt those habits that will work for you. This might mean changing some habits, perhaps getting an earlier start on the day and putting extra time and effort into your tasks. I call this extra time and effort the "extra 10 percent."

The Extra 10 Percent

Olympic sporting events are sometimes won by a fraction of a second. Each competitor is in top performing condition, yet only a few can place as medalists. The subtlest advantage may be needed to win. Perhaps the difference is affected not only by what happens on the day of the event, but what has happened during the years preparing for the event. Have the winning athletes been doing things differently than the ones who could have been winners?

A friend and associate of mine, Henry Marsh, is an inspiration to me because of how he approaches his goals: He is focused, driven, and always makes the extra effort. That is why he has achieved great success in many areas of his life.

Henry Marsh has competed on four consecutive Olympic teams in men's track and field; he was ranked number one in the world three times in *Track & Field News*. He is the current U.S. record holder in the men's 3,000-meter steeplechase and has been for fifteen consecutive years. Henry is also an attorney and published author. I asked him what it is that distinguishes him from other athletes—and other people.

He told me that he went about his training a little differently than most of the other runners. While they trained harder and harder, which was the common approach, he found something different that seemed to get better results. He said:

"First of all, I focused not only on the training but on recovery time as well. While many runners ran themselves into the ground, training very hard, I was training smart. I focused on the workout, the psychology of victory, and what to do during times of recovery. I took some *extra* time to watch, observe, and speak with other champions. I found a successful balance of all these components that allowed me to preform better at the events.

"I also was big on planning. Every Sunday night I would call my coach, Bill Bowerman, the coach of the U.S. Olympic Team in Munich in 1972 and a co-founder of Nike. We would very carefully plan out my training routine for the week and schedule in the recovery time—those *extra* hours on the phone made all of the difference. We were very specific and focused about our strategy—that is what helped me reach my potential as an athlete."

And so it is in life. How many times have you read articles about successful people who had a creative approach to their strategy? How many people have you heard about who did things despite the common belief or the traditional approach? Winners aren't afraid of being different or giving it that little extra effort to fully reach their potential.

From the Track to Every Day

We know grade-point averages and success on exams can be affected by study habits. If we expect to excel in school, we need to add the extra 10 percent. If passing the exam requires about four hours of preparation and study, ensure a good grade by adding 10 percent: An extra thirty minutes of study, one more review session, or a visit to the professor. Little details like these can make enough of a difference at exam time to distinguish you from the rest of the class.

Some businesses offer similar products and services (AT&T and MCI; Coke and Pepsi; most of the major airlines). As a way to recruit and keep your business, they must find subtle ways to find you and develop a relationship. It requires them to add the extra 10 percent.

The extra 10 percent could mean more product in the package, or 10 percent lower rates (in this case, subtracting 10 per-

cent). It could mean 10 percent more
peanuts on the airplanes (yeah!), 10
percent more free long-distance calls.
Any business has the potential to produce fewer defects, have less turnover,

A man is a lion in his own
cause.

Scottish proverb

send more thank-you notes, have more efficient delivery service,
or have a more responsive customer service department. Look at
the average pattern, or even the best pattern, and improve the
process by a few percentage points by making extra efforts where
possible. It may only be a slight difference, but enough for you to
discover some of your true potential as an individual and organization to distinguish yourself from the pack.

As individuals, if most of our business associates arrive at eight
and leave at five, we can add an extra thirty minutes to an hour.
Arrive early, plan the day, organize some personal business. Take
those few moments that others may not be willing to take—it
will make all the difference in your productivity.

If you expect to excel financially, add the extra 10 percent. If
you invest your savings at 10 percent each year, with compounded
interest, that money will double in 7.2 years. If you have a little
better investment plan and could earn 15 percent, that same
investment, with compounded interest, will double in 4.8 years.
Having added a few percentage points brings significantly
improved results over time. And so it is with your behavior and
performance.

You have reservoirs of potential inside you that can only be uti-
lized if you are willing to make the extra effort. And making that
extra effort will require you at times to act alone. You may not be
able to involve everyone in your new change in strategy. If you
place your new ideas and work ethic before your social "House
and Senate," you will rarely get the green light from everybody.
Individuality and going the extra mile can make the difference
between staying in a comfort zone of mediocrity and fully developing your potential.

Thomas Edison, for example, was well known by his peers as a
failure. Because he went against the grain and tried experiments

that seemed useless and impractical, he had plenty of contemporaries that shook their heads in complete bewilderment about what he was thinking as he spent time and wasted thousands of dollars pursuing the completion of inventions like the light bulb and the phonograph.

Edison knew his pursuits were valid and would one day be of use. He stuck to his beliefs, especially through all of his failures, certain that he was doing the right thing and that his efforts would soon be appreciated. He experienced ten thousand failures before creating the functional light bulb, and with each failure he chose to see it as a learning experience. According to the law of averages, one more failure put him one more step toward an impending success. Everyone remembers Thomas Edison; very few can name his contemporaries or his detractors.

At times we, too, must believe in ourselves, follow our heart, and trust the fact that our motives are reason enough to pursue our dreams. Our beliefs are stronger and more valid than other people's thoughts and comments.

Defying the Odds

Aren't you glad . . .

. . . that Roger Bannister didn't buy into the belief that running a four-minute mile is impossible? Although most people couldn't do it, and experts said it was impossible, Roger had his own set of standards. On May 6, 1954, Roger Bannister became the first man in recorded history to run a mile in less than four minutes.

. . . that Orville and Wilbur Wright didn't listen to the scientifically held belief that "heavier-than-air flying machines would never work."? After many months of trial, error, and invention, they finally conducted their first fifty-nine-second flight. On December 17, 1903, the Wright brothers saw their dream become a reality and changed the course of history.

. . . that Wilma Rudolph, a young girl stricken with polio and twice afflicted with double pneumonia, would walk without braces and have a normal childhood? Rudolph overcame her disability, played high-school basketball, and became a track and field champion. In 1960, she won three gold medals at the Olympic games in Rome, Italy—she was also the

> Tell me the company, and I will tell thee what thou art.
> MIGUEL DE CERVANTES

first woman to win three gold medals in track and field.

. . . that Steven Jobs, founder of Apple Computer, didn't listen to most computer executives when presenting the idea of a personal computer. The concept of having a home computer was considered ridiculous. In 1943 Tom Watson, chairman of IBM, said, "I think there is a world market for about five computers." And in 1977, Ken Olsen, president of Digital Equipment Corporation said, "There is no reason for any individual to have a computer in their home."

Hindsight shows that many times the common belief was incorrect, and today we admire and respect those individuals who stuck to their dreams. With patience and determination, they took the "road less traveled" and succeeded.

The road to tapping your potential may require you to defy the odds.

Action Items

- Create your own individualized plan for success—in writing.
- Consider an aspect of your life where you could make an additional ten percent effort to get better results.
- Keep popular figures in mind as motivators and reminders that out-of-the-ordinary things can and do happen.

BELIEFS

Great men are said to have four things
in common: they speak softly, have
the capacity for hard work, a deep
conviction for their cause, and a
consuming belief in their ability to do it.

JOHN D. HESS

When attempting to make changes in your life, you must remember that only you can do it for yourself. You must take full responsibility for your actions and decisions. So before you attempt to work on changing some of your *circumstances*, you should first look at the *source* of actions and decisions—your *beliefs*. You need to act on or emphasize the beliefs that are constructive, those that will help you tap your potential.

There is a tendency to blame external circumstances for the way we are—to justify behavior by characteristics we believe are in our genes, environment, the economy, or a "personal tradition" of having events turn out a certain way. This is a shirking of the responsibility we have to control our own behavior and make decisions that contribute to the life we want to lead. There must be a shift in focus: Rather than find reasons to justify actions or results, we can choose *beliefs* and *habits* that will create better *circumstances* in our lives.

Taking Responsibility

Only you can tap your potential. You cannot send away for success. Nobody can bestow the gift of self-improvement to anyone else. You do not inherit success, you create it. As president, CEO, and administrative assistant of your own future, only you can create and manage what you want. You must consciously decide what goals you will pursue and what beliefs will serve you best in your endeavors.

Many people who have pursued and successfully attained uncommon feats in life faced severe challenges. For example, on July 23, 1989, Greg LeMonde won the Tour de France after a near-death hunting accident just two years before the race. Greg was accidentally struck by his brother-in-law's shotgun blast and hit with sixty number-two-sized pellets. Many pellets were removed in surgery, but when he won the Tour de France, he had thirty pellets still in his body—two of them in his heart. That's a man who believed he would win despite any past personal crisis.

Or take the case of Jim Abbott, who has been a starting pitcher for the California Angels and the New York Yankees. He was a great baseball player in school and actually skipped the minor leagues and played for the majors. He believed he would one day succeed, and he did finally become a baseball star. Jim Abbott was born with only a left arm.

These people confronted some significant challenges, yet assumed the the responsibility of making changes and getting started themselves. They did not feel that the "hand they were dealt in life" was at all permanent. They may have had some assistance from others, but they could not afford to wait for other people to "fix" their situation. They knew what they wanted and had reason to believe it was possible for them. We, to a lesser degree, have similar challenges and the same responsibility to focus on possibilities through constructive beliefs.

In all of my readings and research on the subject of personal development, a message consistently emphasized as critical in the success formula is the importance of how we think. From the Bible's "as a man thinketh in his heart, so is he," to Napoleon Hill's "if you can conceive it and believe it, you can achieve it," there is always a strong case made for maintaining positive beliefs that will contribute to our life's purpose: You are the keeper, editor, owner of everything you hold in your belief system.

Some positive beliefs are:

- I can do anything I put my mind to doing.
- We live in the best of times.
- Tomorrow will bring new opportunities.

Contrast these with some negative beliefs:

- Things never go right for me.
- I think we may be having another recession.
- Tomorrow ought to be a complete disaster.

You must choose the beliefs that will help you in your desire to tap your potential.

Are You Sold on Yourself?

People who are highly motivated to succeed make decisions with one-hundred-percent conviction. Their determination is intense, and they believe they will succeed. They focus on those abilities that will make their dreams a reality. Focusing on perceived negatives in life is misleading and counterproductive. Tapping your potential requires you to focus on the talents and qualities that you have and believe that those qualities are ingredients for success. And if you feel you are missing a few ingredients, you know that you have the wherewithal to acquire what you need. Your success will be determined by your ability to fully utilize your talents and your acquired knowledge—all fueled by positive beliefs in your ability to get what you want.

Let's look at how our beliefs about ourselves and the world around us can affect our ability to tap our potential.

Moments after birth we began to experience planet Earth. We've had our great moments, our tears, our bumps on the head, and our home-runs. We have evolved into the person we are today because of the aggregate impact these experiences have had on us. Our behavior today is influenced by the sum-total of experiences we have had from birth until this moment.

Webster's dictionary defines a belief as "a conviction that certain things are true." These beliefs cannot be seen; they reveal themselves to us through behavior and attitude. We are convinced that certain things are true because we experienced them and need no more proof than our own past experience. Unfortunately sometimes a single experience can "poison the well" and deter us from ever trying some things again. If we had a bad initial experience playing golf, we may *never* pick up a club again.

This can be inhibitive if some past experiences created negative beliefs that limit your potential. You may have tried goal setting, tried getting organized, tried using a planning system, tried changing old habits, or tried getting into shape. If they didn't work out the first time, they probably left a bad impression and prevented any future attempts.

You have filed them away in your memories and now feel a certain way about each past event. In terms of your performance, for example, you may have learned

- I'm not good with details.
- I'm uncoordinated.
- I get nervous speaking in front of a group.
- I'm not very good with new technology.
- I'm not good with computers.

The significance of these events is that your recollection and perception of them is what you will use as reference cards to make future decisions. Imagine! You may rely on your third-grade public-speaking experience as a basis for whether or not you should speak next month. In other words, you have been *conditioned* to believe things about yourself and the world around you.

Although many conditions have changed since the original event (the third-grade speech), you still assume it to be true for you today. It only took a single experience for you, as a child, to believe that it will always be that way. You can eliminate those inhibitive beliefs by applying yourself today with the belief that your past does not define your future.

The Domino Effect

If you stepped back and were able to study all of our opinions about our past performance and behavior, we would make judgments about who we are—this is the basis for our self-image. If we like what we see (or even if we don't), these feelings become the basis for our self-esteem. And depending on how we esteem ourselves, we will create an expectation for what we are capable of achieving in life. If we have average self-esteem, we feel we can only get average results for our efforts—making above-average performance seem unlikely.

Brian Tracey, a world-class motivational speaker, has said that "people rarely exceed their own self-image." We can never underestimate the significance of experience and belief. There is a domino effect beginning with the initial experience that ultimately impacts our self-expectancy—the degree to which you can tap your potential.

Beliefs and Their Impact on Behavior

People who purchase only foreign cars may have a belief about the quality or performance of American-made cars versus those of another country. Or it could be a belief about the status of individuals who drive cars from Germany or Italy.

People who exercise regularly may have a belief that looking good is important or that exercise increases stamina and life span.

People who actively pursue self-improvement and want to learn about making more of their lives believe that there are many opportunities and potentials in this world that are within reach.

If beliefs are the gateway to the quality of performance, you must carefully edit and refine what is in your belief system because of the impact it has on your behavior.

There are so many factors that play a part in the development of your beliefs and conditioning that it is difficult to pinpoint single factors that determine why you are the way you are. But it is safe to say that we are all products of our environment, and your behavior today is a distillation of the many, many experiences you have had. And although it may not be possible to change historical events in your life, it is always possible to change how you perceive them, how you internalize them, and how you allow them to impact your behavior today.

Where Did You Get That Idea?

Behind every failure or success, and for every goal that has been achieved or only dreamed about, there was a belief that influenced the final outcome. You tried and tried because you were sure you could succeed, or you never got started because you didn't believe you could achieve; you buckled down because you thought "time was of the essence"; or you slacked off because you felt there was no real urgency, and "if it was meant to be, then it will happen for me." Circumstances in your life can be a result of your beliefs.

Experiential Versus Inherited Beliefs

As a child, if you touched a hot stove, you learned firsthand (no pun) that it hurts. If someone told you that the winters are cold in China, you acquired that belief from someone else (assuming

you didn't fly there to confirm). You
will be careful not to go near the
stove, and you will wait until the
spring to fly to China. The beliefs

were acquired differently, yet both had their influence on your
behavior. These may be simple examples, but the same process is
at work with the other beliefs that impact our performance at the
office and at home.

Beliefs alone are not harmful unless they influence or create a
behavior pattern that conflicts with our best interests, or they
limit, rather than liberate, our potential.

That Helps/That Hurts

True or false beliefs become significant in the growth process
when they modify behavior and prove themselves to be constructive or inhibitive. If you harbor self-defeating beliefs about the
world and in it our ability to survive, you are tugging along a lot
of psychological baggage. It becomes the intellectual junk food to
an otherwise fit mentality.

Constructive beliefs encourage us to tap our potential and
contribute to our ability to persevere. Some constructive beliefs
might be:

- I have the talent to do whatever is necessary.
- I always manage to persevere.
- Once I learn the ropes, I can be the best.
- With a little patience, I can succeed.
- I'm as good as the next guy.

These beliefs foster and nurture our efforts by the healthy
"internal advice" they provide.

Inhibitive beliefs instill a sense of futility about tapping our
potential, and detract from our desire to persevere. Inhibitive
beliefs can be:

- I can't function unless I get my eight hours rest.
- I can't think without my first cup of coffee.
- It's just my luck that. . . .
- I never win contests.
- If only I had more time.

These undermine, frustrate, and squelch your efforts by the "internal" mis-information they provide.

Your Belief Card-File System

Picture your belief system as a card catalogue system in a library. Everyone has an invisible, alphabetized card-file system of beliefs that he or she assumes to be true. On the front of the card is the subject and what you believe to be true. On the back of the card, you'll find the belief's corresponding behavior pattern.

When you were a child you saw a dog, then ran over to pet its head and were bitten on the hand—ouch! You wrote on the front

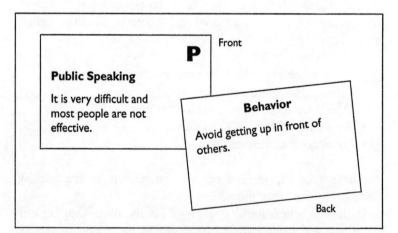

Belief Card-File System: Alphabetized cards with important events in your life and the corresponding behavior on the reverse side of the card.

of a blank card under *D* for Dog that "dogs bite." And on the back of the card, the corresponding behavior becomes, "avoid dogs"!

This statement is true for *you* because *you* experienced it. You refer back to the card with lightening speed each time you see a dog and you act accordingly. It will take a different experience for you to change the belief. If you pet a friendly dog, the belief may be modified to "not *all* dogs bite," and the behavior will follow: "I'll pet *some* dogs."

If you were handed a guitar in the fourth grade and fumbled with it for an hour of noise, you reached into the file under *G* and on the Guitar card wrote "this thing is impossible!" "And on the reverse of the card: "Try something other than the guitar."

If you believe that playing the violin requires a touch of genius you don't have, you never take the first lesson.

The violin example may not have been your experience; you may have acquired it from somebody else. It is possible that one day a friend mentioned in passing (and under her breath) that the violin is a tough instrument to learn. And as she said it, she reached into your personal card-file system and wrote on the card under *V*—Violin: "Unless you're a genius, don't bother"—and you have referred to it from that day forward.

If you believe that walking under a ladder is bad luck and carrying a rabbit's foot is good luck, you may act accordingly. People have beliefs and superstitions about a lot of things: the number thirteen, spilling salt, black cats, finding a lucky penny. The interesting part about superstition and belief is that, regardless of whether or not there is any truth to them, people act as if they are true and will create the expected circumstances themselves. If you expect to have an unlucky Friday the thirteenth, you see only the evil. If you look for the good on the day you found the penny, you'll keep score of the blessings. Therefore, we could also suggest that our beliefs influence what we see in the world.

The question becomes whether or not what has been recorded and filed away in our belief system are going to serve our best interests—are they constructive? False beliefs can hinder our potential if they are in any way limiting. For example, if we believe that we'll always be late for meetings, if we believe we can't get organized, and if we believe that a poor grade-point average in school predetermines much of our future success, we limit our potential. All of these beliefs would lead to behaviors or actions that undermine and hurt the endeavor we have to be our best—we may never tap our potential because we don't attempt to be on time, don't clean our desk, etc. We don't know how good we could be because the inhibitive belief stops us from applying ourselves in the first place.

What do you believe about your ability to

- become president?
- make a million dollars?
- learn a foreign language?
- write a book?

Remember that other people's opinions do not have to become yours. They have had a very different introduction into this world than you have had, and so they refer to a very different belief card-file system. You become the final judge in determining if you want to subscribe to the belief and make room for it in your file system. You must always judge for yourself if what you are hearing is

1. true.
2. true in all cases.
3. true for you in your life.

You may have a couple of natural talents that would make the violin, the guitar, or writing a book an easy endeavor.

Modify Before You File

You can consciously modify the beliefs or the corresponding behavior in your belief card-file system. For example, if you heard that law school is tough, rather than not pursue the degree, you might decide to focus on what would make the degree attainable. Instead of thinking, "I'll get a job instead," you may think, "Therefore I'll work diligently, apply myself, develop a specific success strategy for graduating from law school."

You can replace inhibitive thoughts with more constructive ones. You can replace "the violin is impossible" with "the violin is stimulating and exciting." You turn negatives into positives, obstacles into opportunities, and frustration into positive energy when you *internalize* the *external* events in ways that will help, not hinder.

Or you could change the belief itself. Instead of saying, "Law school is tough," you can modify it to "law school is challenging." Problems become opportunities and risk becomes adventure if you file beliefs away so it encourages rather than defeats your efforts.

Once you recognize that your actions are tied to beliefs, you should subscribe to those beliefs that encourage you to take initiative and achieve. Your ability to tap your potential will be largely determined by whether or not you think you can. Henry Ford said it best in the 1930s: "If you think you can or you can't, you're probably right." You must replace all negative beliefs and focus on creating positive beliefs. There is no room for the excess psychological baggage that literally weighs you down and stands between you and your goals. There are enough challenges that accompany career advancement, financial success, and balancing priorities without having the burden and added weight of negative beliefs about yourself, your world, and your potential, which would deny you the very things you so much desire.

Success Stories

Seminars and books that teach skills development never work for those who simultaneously concentrate on reasons why the concepts may not work. You can't dabble in the idea of tapping potential as a skeptic or hesitate because of doubt and fear. You must jump in with both feet. History and human example demonstrate that people's success is not necessarily built upon physical, genealogical, or intellectual abilities. People tap their potential and become the best at what they do because they focus on possibilities, action, and purpose.

For example, did you realize that the following successes have, or had, learning disabilities?

Tom Cruise—Hollywood film star
Bruce Jenner—1976 Olympic gold medalist
Hans Christian Anderson—writer of children's stories
Nelson Rockefeller—industrialist
Woodrow Wilson—U. S. President
Leonardo da Vinci—Renaissance artist and inventor

Did you know that the following successes never finished high school?

Walt Disney—film creator and businessman
George Gershwin—award-winning composer
Will Rogers—humorist
The Wright brothers—inventors
Peter Jennings—TV anchorman

Did you know that the following successes never finished grade school?

Benjamin Franklin—statesman, author, inventor, writer
Mark Twain—author, humorist
Charles Dickens—author
Claude Monet—artist

These are examples of people who had potential and developed it to its fullest—regardless of other people's opinions and despite personal characteristics that they could have perceived as roadblocks to success.

For example, Claude Monet, given his training and ideas, was ridiculed. He and his fellow Impressionists were banned from popular salon exhibitions for years. Today we love their works of art, but at the time only they believed that these works carried any artistic value. One critic wrote "five or six lunatics . . . have joined to show their work." It took a full ten years of work and exposure before Impressionists and their artwork were accepted.

And what about baseball legend Babe Ruth? His lifetime batting average was .342. Impressed? Have you considered what that represents about the importance of dealing with failure? A .342 batting average means that about two-thirds of the time at bat, he left the plate disappointed. He only found success about one in every three visits to the plate! If you focus on what you want in life with great intensity—to the point that failing two-thirds of the time doesn't affect you—how much more potential could you tap?

Achievement is like climbing a ladder: if you're worried about falling or what's beneath you, you stop climbing and the fear of falling leaves you paralyzed.

All of the aforementioned successes achieved their dreams through diligence, coaching from others, and a constant belief that they would eventually succeed. Successful people are willing and able, especially in the face of adversity, to talk themselves through the difficulties and reach the objectives. You cannot simultaneously consider the reasons why and why not success is possible. You can't have it both ways.

I Gave at the Office, Too!

Businesses survive and prosper because managers collect the talents of employees and use a variety of backgrounds and experience to reach a common end. All people involved must be focused on the common objective(s) and *believe* that all challenges can be met and all obstacles overcome. Everyone must feed and foster the self-esteem around the office, be of help and support wherever possible, become a resource for others, and make many other contributions, big and small, that will serve the organization's mission.

If doubt, low morale, a belief that "we don't count," or "we don't make a difference," or burnout sets in at the office, look out! Companies cannot afford to have feelings of ambivalence about its ability to increase profitability or market share. There must be a positive sense of optimism about their ability to succeed. Just like any team effort, whether it is a football team, a cast in a play, or a one-hundred-piece orchestra, it is essential that all understand their unique roles, the group's objective, and *believe* that success is a sure thing.

In order to tap the potential of the organization, you must first tap the potential of its employees.

I have had many people in closed-door meetings confide in me that the "real problem around here is"—and then they almost whisper the *problem du jour* around the company—ego, dishonesty, politics, incompetence on the part of so-and-so, tardiness, poorly run meetings, poorly planned days, or people having "sleepers" at the office because of their happy hour on Tuesday that snowballed into an all-night affair. In other words, some personal imperfections are manifesting themselves in a professional setting.

This is not to suggest that companies will ever be free of all of these challenges, but I will suggest that these setbacks emanate from individuals not having a positive approach to their priorities, or perhaps not having constructive beliefs that things could change for the better if they applied themselves. In this case, a way to get better results in the company is to strengthen the roots (the individuals) by changing some beliefs and behaviors.

That is one of the more important elements in understanding the significance of personal improvement: Every organization is composed of the same thing—people. All companies are nothing more than a bunch of real, living, breathing, human beings with needs and dreams. To improve the lives of the very fiber of the company is to improve the company itself. That is why personal and professional development is given so much attention at most companies. If companies can get constructive belief systems in place with its employees, everything else comes easily.

Corporate attitudes and beliefs have the ability to build an empire or destroy an otherwise good company. If you started your own company, would you hire ten optimists or ten pessimists? Save your money; Three optimists can do the work of ten pessimists.

Your Past Has No Bearing on Your Future

It is not who your parents are, whether you are male or female, how tall or short you are, or in what neighborhood you were raised. Being an Aquarius, a Leo, right-brained, visual, Italian, Type A, or bald need not be thought of as a significant determining factor in your success. These are external factors that can have an effect on you only if you let them; external events are only a problem if you allow them to be mis-internalized. Part of your success in tapping your potential will be created through your ability to "clear the slate" of old, inhibitive, false beliefs and perceptions about yourself and the world around you.

> The mind is its own place, and in itself can make a heav'n of hell, a hell of heav'n.
>
> JOHN MILTON

In your card-file system under S for Success, I'd like you to file the following: "You can have it all if only you tap your potential."

At a seminar I was teaching in Los Angeles, a woman approached me and said she wasn't sure if she could apply the concepts I had just discussed:

"I'm not sure that some of these ideas will work for me," she stated.

"How do you know?"

"Well, I'm not sure you can teach an old dog new tricks—plus I'm a middle child."

At this point I was sure I had more than I had bargained for.

"Well," I said cautiously, "I think breaking old habits and acquiring some new ones may take time, but what does being a middle child have to do with trying new things?"

"Oh, you know what they say: 'There's a little rebellion in all middle children.'"

(Behind *M* for Middle children: "They are rebellious"—and the corresponding behavior: "Although everyone has attended the program to improve, rebel against instruction for the sake of being different.)"

I had to pretend that I had heard that one before but tried to get the message across that if she fails in life or if she succeeds, the number in line she happens to be in the family tree would not be a determining factor. Only she can make decisions for herself now; she is responsible for letting that belief interfere with her potential.

From Positive Thinking to Constructive Beliefs

Positive thinking has been sold as a major element in the success ideal. I don't think it is. Looking on the bright side, a positive mental attitude and optimism are only ingredients. I meet people every day who are sure that things will "soon change for the better," that everything will "work itself out," and "all you gotta have is faith." This is true, but not without effort on the part of the individual. It is easy to look up and ask for a little assistance; it is a challenge to reinforce that hope by buckling down and getting started on a project. Attitude will breathe the life into good plans and goals. It's the difference between saying "Have a great day!" versus, "You'll do a great job in today's meeting." The latter is clearly more specific and focused. A constructive belief will support your optimism in a specific endeavor—it empowers your ability to find solutions. Positive thinking is more vague—it relieves stress.

Sometimes we fall into the trap of putting our energies into our thoughts instead of our actions. We hope and pray that our *desire* will make things happen, regardless of whether or not we take some *action*. We giggle at how long we procrastinate life's little

> In the province of the mind, what one believes to be true is either true, or becomes true.
>
> JOHN LILLY

responsibilities but actually feel a bit of guilt about our inability to fix the problem. We must remember the secret ingredients for results: attitude + action.

You shouldn't empower negative beliefs regarding your circumstances. Careful renovation of these beliefs will allow you to disempower and discard obstacles to your success.

You may have read "Waiting for Godot" by the great Irish playwright, Samuel Beckett. The existential drama explores many aspects of human nature and morality. Aside from the humor and absurdity of the characters, there is the prevalent theme of inaction on the part of the main characters, Vladimir and Estragon. The final scene summarizes the characters' paralysis throughout the entire play:

ESTRAGON: Well? Shall we go?
VLADIMIR: Pull on your trousers.
ESTRAGON: What?
VLADIMIR: Pull on your trousers.
ESTRAGON: You want me to pull off my trousers?
VLADIMIR: Pull ON your trousers.
ESTRAGON: (*Realizing his trousers are down*). True. (*He pulls up his trousers.*)
VLADIMIR: Well? Shall we go?
ESTRAGON: Yes, let's go.

(*They do not move.*)

Curtain

Although you are not as outlandish as the characters in his play, you have probably behaved in similar ways: preparing, talking, and thinking about the future and where you may be going, but actually going nowhere. Good intentions must be paired with good implementation if you want results.

Remaining optimistic about a future that has not been addressed by today's daily actions bears no fruit. Working toward a particular end and remaining optimistic along the way with constructive beliefs will significantly increase your ability to persevere. The important thing to remember is that "constructive thinking," coupled with consistent actions, is what will make a difference.

Beliefs and behavior have a cause-and-effect relationship. The focus of the next chapter will discuss fine tuning your behavior toward a specific purpose.

The combination of constructive beliefs and consistent action make tapping your potential possible.

Action Items

- Eliminate inhibitive beliefs that block your ability to tap potential.
- Consciously try to correct negative self-talk with the more positive alternative.
- Identify a change that can be made in your life (get better organized, for example) that starts with your attitude, then calendar the activity to ensure that you follow through.

PURPOSE

Where there is no vision, the people perish.

PROV. 29:18

Alfred Lord Tennyson, one of my favorite Victorian poets has long been considered a poet of the people. I have spent many hours reading his great works, and a poem that comes to mind when I feel as if I am going through the motions of my daily routine without a sense of purpose or reason is "The Charge of the Light Brigade."

In this poem he dramatizes the true story of a British cavalry during the Crimean War. The cavalry received some confusing orders that led them into a wall of Russian artillery and cost the lives of three-fourths of the 600 horsemen engaged in the attack. Although the troops had mixed feelings about marching "into the valley of death," they never questioned the command:

> Was there a man dismayed?
> Not though the soldier knew
> Someone had blundered.
> Theirs not to make reply,
> Theirs not to reason why,
> Theirs but to do and die.
> Into the valley of death
> Rode the six hundred.

What was it like to march forward into a predicament of fatal risks and certain danger? How confident and committed would you have been? Would some lives been spared if they had a greater sense of purpose? Probably, yes.

We all face risks and challenges in life, but if we have a strong sense of purpose and are tenacious we will be better able to beat the odds and succeed; and if we do encounter obstacles, we will not be discouraged. We will regard our defeat as a temporary challenge along the path of victory.

I have had employers tell me to do something and to not ask questions. To write a report, make a series of phone calls, or attend a meeting without knowing why or what purpose it served always filled me with doubt, tentativeness, and apathy. There is nothing more counterproductive than feelings of futility about what we do in our lives.

We can eliminate the doubt and futility in our daily routines and replace it with *purpose* by creating plans tied to our goals—both of which serve a meaningful purpose. Our daily activities should not be expenditures of time; they should be investments. Exercise should contribute to your fitness goals; meetings held should contribute to reaching departmental goals; saving money should contribute to a financial plan for retirement. Performing tasks that are tied to goals is an important part of tapping our potential; if there is a desire to accomplish goals, we need to streamline or "funnel" tasks and time toward the objective.

For best results, take about twenty minutes and record on paper why you feel you go to work, get out of bed each day, etc. It will change how you perceive the value of your daily activities.

Controlling Your Inner Self

Viktor Frankl, an Austrian psychotherapist and author of several books including *Man's Search for Meaning*, writes clearly about the importance of purpose, not only in terms of goal-setting, but as a life-preserving mechanism. To simplify his theory, called logotherapy, he states that without a goal, we die. When we no longer look forward to tomorrow, or when we feel that it doesn't matter if we get out of bed or not, something inside of us dies. Conversely, think about how "alive" we feel when every day has meaning: We have more energy, enthusiasm, and a better attitude. The good news is with a little thought we can discover our purpose and reason for participating in life.

A Jew, Frankl was imprisoned in concentration camps during World War II and miraculously lived to write about it. He lost his family to the gas chambers and was reduced to a number in a prison camp where he was routinely tortured. None of the prisoners knew if he or she could survive the environment. Even if they could survive, it was possible they'd be called away to the ovens. Not much to look forward to on a daily basis.

I read somewhere that "no matter where the body is, the mind is free to wander." That is the power and the choice to which Frankl chose to cling. Anything could happen *to* him, but what happened *inside* of him was his choice and his responsibility. Anything he could do to keep his mind alive and increase his reason for waking each day would serve him well. He turned his camp into his research facility, making little secret notes on paper about his observations and theories. He had to keep his notes hidden for fear that he may be killed for doing any kind of "thinking" for himself.

He noticed that when people's minds gave up, the bodies soon followed. When people realized that they may never leave the horrors of the camp, and if they did they had no money, possessions, or family to turn to, the depression, coupled with extremely poor health, was enough to kill them; they simply walked into a corner, lay down, and died.

On a much more subtle level we benefit (survive) during the day, or we give up (perish) relative to the degree of purpose and determination we have for a particular cause. Having purpose eliminates the distractions in life; lack of purpose allows the distractions to crowd out what should be our focus. Whether we call them our resolutions, goals, dreams, or tasks, it is crucial to have an agenda every day that is a part of a bigger picture: A to-do list that is tied to our goals. The motivation to pursue these objectives is what keeps us healthy and alive.

Purpose gives you the motivation to want to tap your potential.

Mind as Medicine

In the fall of 1989, I was teaching seminars on "Increasing Productivity" in the Northeast. I had been keeping a fairly heavy travel schedule, and it had taken its toll. Between the time changes, the humidity in one city, and the cold in the next; between the air-conditioned hotel rooms to the recirculated air of the long flights and their highly nutritious meals (I complain about the food, but still look forward to seeing that little cart roll my way), I found myself afflicted with the flu.

I was to speak in Boston all day, drive north to New Hampshire for two full-day seminars the following day, then drive south to Connecticut for yet another full-day seminar, and then return to Boston and fly back to Los Angeles. There was a lot of work to be done (250 total seminar participants to teach), and there were no substitutes to take my place at that time—there would be no option for "calling in sick."

I was forced to put my mind to getting better. I tried to stay mentally tough. I never admitted to myself that I had the flu, I drank lots of fluids, took lots of vitamin C, catnapped at the lunch hour, ate all the right foods. My mission was to get through the week without a hitch and never let the audience have a clue about the misery I was feeling. I had a great sense of purpose and no time for the flu. Although I had contemplated wearing a bathrobe and slippers to the seminar, I felt it might be a distraction.

I remember having to pull over at a rest stop to sleep for a half hour to revive myself after the busy day. I also remember having the flu symptoms get worse at the end of the day. I attributed this to allowing my guard to drop; I knew it was okay to "be sick" and so, psychologically, I welcomed the problems into my evening. I persevered, and the week was a success because the illness never took hold of me the way it normally would. I was absolutely determined to beat the flu, and I did. I was actually too busy to be sick.

Purpose can be stronger than disease and is life-sustaining.

Have you ever been depressed? Does depression raise or lower your immune system? Of course, it lowers it. A personal tragedy can temporarily impact your natural defenses against common viruses. When you lack purpose and laze around the house all day watching television, you still feel tired. It doesn't matter that you've had ten hours of sleep and two half-hour naps, you're still exhausted at the end of the day. Then the phone rings—you get invited to an event you wouldn't miss for the world, and inexplicable energy surfaces. You are happier, your self-esteem skyrockets, and you forget about life's little troubles. Having something to look forward to turns everything around: You feel alive and you feel the blood circulate again. Therefore, it is critical that you find and create goals in life worth fighting for. It is good for you physically and mentally.

Lack of purpose takes a toll, having purpose taps your reservoirs of energy.

Retired? Rethink!

I once was asked to speak at a retirement home. I accepted. Then I realized I would be standing in front of twenty-five septuagenarians telling them to tap their potential, set goals, etc. I wasn't sure how receptive they would be to this message. But the more I thought about it, the more I realized that goals almost become more important as we get older, that having a sense of purpose at age eighty is as important as at age eighteen, so I prepared the speech.

As I entered the home, I had no idea what I would face in the lecture because of the many people sitting in chairs sleeping, whispering quietly amongst themselves, and wheeling each other through the lobby. I was surprised to find that a sincerely interested group attended the session, and after I had finished, many people present chimed in with a bunch of "Amens" and personal stories that supported the importance of my message. They were all students of these philosophies and knew intimately the life-preserving qualities that plans, goals, and involvement can have.

They told me that all their lives they were expected to be somewhere; they had numerous responsibilities including their families, jobs, and a whole host of accountibilities that kept them occupied. They had a reason to get out of bed and a purpose in their day. Once they retired and reached seventy-five and older, they became responsible for creating their own sense of accountability to others.

They elaborated on the importance of volunteer work. They all belonged to clubs or organizations. Whether it was bingo, sewing class, ballroom dancing, gardening, singing and music, or the periodic trip to Las Vegas, they all had something to look forward to. They demonstrated Maxwell Maltz's theory in his classic work *Psychocybernetics* that "people are like bicycles: If they are not moving in a particular direction, they fall over." As a means of survival, and to increase the quality and variety in their lives, they stay busy. What can we learn from our elders?

Staying Involved

Studies have shown that people who have had highly productive lives in business and civil service need to stay busy when they retire, or they risk an early death. It is very difficult to shift from a constructive daily schedule to watering the garden and watching television. This can lower self-esteem, and, as previously

mentioned, cause a part of our spirit
to die as well. The self-image can
change from being a valued contribu-
tor in the world to feeling like excess
baggage siphoning off the contribu-
tors. We miss playing on a team.

> The grand essentials to hap-
> piness are something to do,
> someone to love, and some-
> thing to hope for.
> JOSEPH ADDISON

We've all heard the problems some
families face in "what to do with grandma" as she gets shifted
among relatives, babysat by different people, and moved into a
home. She needs help in and out of doors and with other routine
tasks, which affects her dignity. Those in their "golden years"
know exactly what is going on, and their self-image and self-
esteem plummet; and at that age, the effects can be sad and serious. It doesn't matter how old you are, you need a sense of
community, self-worth, and involvement.

Missing the Connection

Most organizations today have a printed vision statement—they
know where they would like to be in the years to come. They
also have a mission statement—they know what their particular
business objectives are in the world, in the industry, and within
their product line. They also have a list of corporate values—they
know how to behave as a group in order to make the mission and
vision a reality. You forget that those one-page statements are so
powerful they can guide a company with thousands of employees. What would happen if you wrote one for yourself? Writing a
mission statement will detail what you feel to be your purpose in
life, your reason for taking part in the human race. If you can discover ways to make a difference on this planet, you change from
perceiving yourself as drifting through life minding only your
immediate business to feeling a sense of stewardship for others
and their well-being. The latter is much more gratifying and will
have positive ramifications in all aspects of your lives. Do you
have responsibilities and accountibilities to others? Are you here

to entertain, inform, nurture, counsel, feed, write, market, help, revitalize, cultivate, gentrify, or serve the world?

The mission statement that you write should be driven by your values. You feel strongly about volunteering, being charitable, advancing a career, etc. The reason you have a mission to start with is because these top priorities in life are waiting to manifest themselves through your actions. This identification process will require only some quiet time, some thought, and a pencil. It is best accomplished as a writing exercise and will prove itself to be highly motivating.

Values will be discussed at greater length later in the book. The importance of mentioning them here is to "prep the soil" for connecting purpose to the *right things* in life. The principles discussed in this book cannot be viewed on a component by component basis. There is a continuity and an inter-dependent nature in all the chapters of *Tapping Potential*, and hindsight will add to your ability to recognize the trees from the forest and see how all the pieces of the puzzle fit together.

Having a solid sense of purpose establishes a reason for tapping your potential.

Action Items

- Create to-do lists that include a task that will contribute to you reaching a goal.
- Identify the talents you have on paper and ask yourself how those will contribute to your purpose.
- Write a mission statement for why you go to work, and why you get out of bed every day.

ATTITUDE

Nothing great was ever achieved
without enthusiasm.

RALPH WALDO EMERSON

In the late 1950s, the significance of attitude in the success formula was widely hailed as the very element that could change it all. Many popular authors over the years have emphasized that a positive attitude along with a little faith could get you some impressive results. The power of a positive mental attitude, of positive thinking, and of a positive outlook has been endorsed over and over again as a critical part of goal achievement and living our dreams, and I believe wholeheartedly in its power.

Your attitude will determine the degree to which you can tap your potential.

However, attitude isn't enough! There must be some *action* on your part! Having a positive attitude about your ability to succeed, without having defined goals, is not enough. Having faith and the right attitude about achieving a goal you are currently pursuing make much more sense and will bring measurable results. Your attitude must manifest itself through specific action if you are to actually accomplish your goals.

You can develop a language of self-talk that creates a winning attitude. When you tell yourself to "keep going, stay with it, and the show must go on" you use a language that creates the focused positive attitude needed to carry out the action and win. As soon as doubt, fear, or a negative attitude takes over, the battle is lost. You somehow sabotage your efforts with something as seemingly harmless as a state of mind.

Choose Your Attitude

As you attempt to add value to your life and unleash the powers you have within, you must develop the habit and ability of choosing the attitude you need at the moment. When things are developing nicely in life, one positive experience builds upon the next, and, with that momentum, you feel unstoppable. But because not every day is a phenomenal success, you need to find ways to throw yourself into character to tap the potential needed at any given moment.

> You can do very little with faith, but you can do nothing without it.
>
> SAMUEL BUTLER

Actors do this all the time. When performing, they may need to change from laughter to tears in a matter of minutes. Although they may be socializing off the set, they may need to become enraged for only a few seconds in a particular scene on camera; the more "convinced" the actors are of their rage, the more we read it on their faces and believe it.

What about the classic "locker-room" speech that inspires, motivates, and creates the desire to perform and win the game? There is a reason why these pep talks take place regularly: They clear the slate of negativity and turn the focus toward a winning *attitude*, which will manifest itself through physical performance.

You are faced with less dramatic but similar challenges. How many times have you had to go from a traffic ticket to a sales presentation, from a failure to an expected success, from a member in an unproductive meeting to a meeting leader at the next? There are many examples of how "getting off to a bad start" or "waking up on the wrong side of the bed" can ruin an entire day. There are also reasons why it doesn't have to: You are responsible for your own attitude. Ben Franklin said that "although we cannot control what goes on in the world around us, we can always control what happens inside of us." We must remember that we don't make a negative event any better by compounding it with a negative attitude. Our only option at that point is to pull ourselves up by our boot straps, dust off, and find the way we can benefit, grow, and learn from the experience.

Where Do You Draw the Line?

Perhaps I should temper the power of the attitude a bit. I would like to re-emphasize, however, that attitude without implementation means nothing. If the Wright brothers only talked about their dream, there would have been no success at Kittyhawk. If they thought positively about the concept but didn't actually implement it, nothing would have been produced. It was the right attitude plus actions that got results.

Does having a great attitude guarantee us *everything*? The likelihood of me becoming a ballet dancer is slim. I probably won't be a rocket scientist or a chess champion. And I say I won't because of two reasons: desire and talent. These aren't important to me; these are not my passions. And my background and areas of formal study make rocket-science expertise a long shot. My current lack of understanding and talent on the chessboard also make it improbable. But with a good attitude I could dig a little deeper and uncover my potential. A positive attitude will prepare you to achieve and enable you to improve your efforts; but, you must take the right kinds of actions that move you toward your goal.

If I attended a two-week chess camp, I'd return a better player. My ability to be a champion is still unknown, but my ability to *improve* is measurable. If I sign up for the camp and study with enthusiasm and practice diligently, I'm sure to do better. Most of us in life are not looking to become champions—our potential can be improved and appreciated by doing many little things through applying ourselves. And it is the attitude that either propels us in the right direction, or discourages us at the outset.

Your Attitude Is Contagious

I remember once a young boy rang my doorbell selling candy bars for a particular cause. Naturally, his selling skills weren't top-notch, but his attitude was exemplary for every sales person in the country.

Sometimes we are approached by people who are not enthusiastic about their cause, and because *they* aren't excited, *we* don't believe that we should be. But every now and then, someone, because of their energy, optimism, and attitude, imbues us with their enthusiasm and excitement. *We buy the person's charisma.*

This particular little boy sold not the candy bar, but the *experience* his summer camp experience promised to offer. He began:

"Hello, my name is Johnny, and I am selling candy bars to pay for expenses at a summer camp where I will learn new things and camp and play baseball and a whole bunch of stuff. It's really fun because you meet lots of kids your own age and get to try new things and stuff like that."

With his eyes dancing and his head nodding he continued to elaborate.

". . . and so to raise money for all this, we need to sell candy bars. Would you want to buy one to help?"

By this time I had trouble holding back my smile as he almost gasped for air after his nonstop presentation. I don't eat candy bars. I never went to summer camp. I bought three candy bars. It didn't matter to me what organization he represented; because he was sincere, enthusiastic, and had a little guts, I had to reward him for the effort. In fact, he made me want to go to summer camp—that's an attitude that's "catching." You can have the same contagious attitude.

Think about how you feel when you hang up the phone after a conversation with a good friend who just received a promotion. The energy in their voice, the optimism about their future, and the conviction in their speech makes us want to do something extraordinary right away. The attitude actually leaves a greater impression on us than the details of the conversation. People hear what you say through your energy and physiology as much or more than what you actually say verbally. You are constantly sending out signals to the rest of the world through nonverbal communication, so at times you must "get into character" to fit the particular situation.

Sometimes tapping your potential will require you to get into character in order to meet some demands.

Experts in communication tell us that if you change your body's posture, the attitude will follow. Chest out, shoulders back, and a little energy will have its effect on attitude. Conversely, it can become difficult to sound interested and energetic on the phone when reclining or lying on the couch.

James Loehr, sports psychologist and author of *Toughness Training for Life,* calls this the "power of 'as if'" principle.

He says:

- How you walk, how you carry your head and shoulders, and the expression on your face can stimulate emotion-specific responses.
- Acting "as if" you feel a particular way can get the chemistry moving in that direction.
- Acting "as if" is a trained response—the more you do it, the better you'll be at making it work.

Try a positive attitude and a positive posture as you attack the day's priorities—it makes a big difference in performance.

I know from experience that speaking to large audiences requires a bit of showmanship. Whether I feel like it or not, I must deliver. It doesn't matter to the group how many miles I have traveled that month, whether or not I have a cold, or if my back hurts, my job is to "become my material." So I mentally throw myself into the state of mind needed to deliver a program with energy, enthusiasm, and conviction. Only then will the audience believe that my message is worth hearing.

You can't tap your potential unless you "feel like it" and are in the right frame of mind needed to draw upon your talents.

Life Is a Laboratory

I invite you to see how different attitudes work in a variety of circumstances throughout the day. This is important to try, not because we want to swindle or mislead others, but to test a theory that can be applied throughout life. Try a positive attitude with people who rarely receive one from others—the sometimes-overlooked people in your daily life.

The next time you get food at a drive-through, make it a point to ask the employee how his or her day is going. You'll see a surprised and grateful look because most people don't take the time to ask the drive-through clerk, the elevator operator, the receptionist, the toll-booth operator, the waiter, the security guard, the grocery bagger, and the hundreds of others you encounter in routine transactions during the day how they are feeling and what kind of day they are having. It is a rare gesture and will be appreciated by the person who may go all day without hearing some expressed gratitude from others.

I feel that it is not only a kind gesture to be pleasant and take special notice of others, but if you ask questions or comment to others with some energy in your voice, you can create and infuse the same attitude in them. People appreciate this, and your kindness will be returned to you in some form, if not by that individual, then in some other way (just one of those inexplicable laws of the universe that says "what comes around, goes around").

You increase your potential, and the potential of others, when setting the stage with a constructive attitude.

Attitude Is a Medicine

As you may already know, there is a significant connection between the wellness of the mind and body. If your thoughts are not well, your body may become ill.

Stress, stored anger, frustrations, anxieties, and any other destructive emotions release chemicals inside us that manifest themselves via arthritis, heart attack, the common cold, and lethargy. The good news is that a healthy attitude, coupled with healthy behaviors, can have an opposite, healing effect.

Dr. Herbert Benson, Harvard M.D., discussed in great detail the mind-body connection. He makes critical points that the body does "overhear" the mind, and it responds accordingly. It hears your pep talks and your criticisms about yourself and life in general. Everything from beliefs to attitudes manifest themselves in the biological make-up of your body, so you need to control and be choosy about the thoughts and attitudes you allow to occupy your mind.

An experiment was conducted at Tufts University involving senior citizens between the ages of eighty-seven and ninety-six. They were a frail group of unenthusiastic, underexercised individuals who needed special help to perform simple tasks, including getting out of bed. Their self-image was one of dependency, and opportunities were limited to the retirement home, not what you would perceive as a group with potential in the world of physical fitness.

According to the study, within eight weeks of the training program "wasted muscles had come back by 300 percent, coordination and balance improved, and an overall sense of active life returned." Doctors agree that to begin exercising at that age, you must *believe* that it will do your body good; you set aside all fears and concerns and you must have faith in yourself. In other words, the healthy attitude is what gets you into the weight room; the rest is just a question of time and discipline. These people had greater potential than they may have figured in improving the quality of their lives, and their lives had more potential and more to offer them if they could motivate themselves out of bed and into the waiting world. The same rule applies to people of all ages and circumstances.

Norman Cousins, in his famous work *The Healing Heart*, provides many insights into the attitude and belief affecting the body. Humor and

Laughter is inner jogging.
NORMAN COUSINS

laughter were his medicine and what he frequently recommended to others. He said, "Laughter was just a metaphor for the entire range of positive emotions. Hope, faith, love, will to live, cheerfulness, humor, creativity, playfulness, confidence, great expectations—all these, I believe, have therapeutic value." A fighting spirit, a will to live, and determination will have one kind of effect on the body—much different than apathy, depression, or resignation.

Wait for the Punchline

One way to maintain a positive outlook on life is to find the humor in every situation. Most of life's difficulties are only to be laughed at later in life anyway, so find the humor today in what will be funny when looking back at it later. That is why comedians are so revered and well paid: They find the humor and the absurdity in daily living and present it as it applies to everyone. Has it ever occurred to you why we all find that style of humor so funny? It's because we share many common experiences—good and bad—and laughter somehow takes the edge off of an otherwise stressful situation.

A good friend and colleague of mine, Greg Fullerton, told me a story about an experience I think about every time I stay at a hotel, every time I order room service, and, especially, every time I think of Greg Fullerton.

With Greg's permission, I have paraphrased the story:

"I was travelling one week and had gone to my room tired at the end of the day and decided to order room service. When the food arrived I set up the little table in the room and had dinner. It felt good to change out of my suit, relax, and watch a little television.

"When I finished eating I decided to put the tray in the hallway so someone from room service could pick it up. Because of the configuration of the inset doorways, I had to push it along the floor a bit further than normal to keep it out of the way. The trick was to s-t-r-e-t-c-h my arms out of the doorway without losing balance, and without letting the door close behind me. As luck would have it I leaned too far forward, almost fell on my face, and lunged forward into the hallway—in my underwear—in order to catch my balance. The worst sound I had heard in my life was the sound of my door: *click*. Actually, that was the second worst sound.

"As I turned around to face my now-closed door, about 200 thoughts per second raced through my mind as to what this would mean for me now, the next ten minutes, and how this may potentially affect my career. My thoughts were broken by the next worst sound: *ding*. The elevator had arrived!

"I prayed that Ray Charles would be its passenger, but it turned out to be an unsuspecting business traveler. He stopped, looked, laughed a bit, and said 'you look like you might be in a bit of trouble.'

"I asked politely if he would do me a favor and call the front desk and get someone to let me back in my room—a male employee if at all possible.

"To complicate the situation, this whole thing happened on a Halloween night. Another miserable sound came from down the hall: a door opening and voices coming closer to me. They stopped, in their costumes for the night, said hello, and asked me what I was doing. I told them, "Nothing, and you?" They said they were going to a party in the lobby and that maybe they would see me down there later. Did they think I was in costume?

"I was eventually let back in my room, and to this day I will not put the room service tray in the hallway unless I drag the dresser in the doorway to prevent the same thing from happening again."

> Man is the only creature endowed with the power of laughter.
>
> FULKE GREVILLE,
> (LORD BROOKE)

When I wiped the tears from my eyes after hearing him tell this story, I realized why Greg is a great success, and why people enjoy being around him: He takes what he *does* seriously, but never *himself* too seriously. He sees the absurdity in life and finds it nothing more than great material for parties and "guess-what-happened-to-me" phone calls. Everyone should have a little of Greg's sense of humor.

Norman Cousins writes, "I emphasized that laughter was only one of the positive emotions . . . and it tends to block deep feelings of apprehension and even panic that all too frequently accompany serious illness. It helps free the body of the constricting effects of the negative emotions that in turn may impair the healing system."

Finding the humor in life is a choice—we decide to look for it and then enjoy it. It somehow makes life's head-on collisions with disappointment nothing more than a brief side-swipe. We feel less burdened by life's challenges and therefore are able to persevere.

You can only tap your potential if you enjoy the process and weather out adversity.

Action Items

- Consciously adopt a positive attitude and positive posture as you attack the day's priorities.
- Remember that sometimes you must "throw yourself into character" to get desired results.
- Experiment with better, more constructive attitudes as you encounter people in so-called routine tasks.

PROACTIVE VERSUS REACTIVE BEHAVIOR

Heaven never helps the men who do not act.

SOPHOCLES

Every day we are faced with a great number of urgencies and demands. There is the fax the must be sent immediately; there are the phone calls that must be returned before we leave for lunch; there are the reports that must be prepared and submitted before the end of the week; and the bills that must be paid by next Friday. And through all of this madness, we somehow rise to the occasion and meet the demands. Some people actually take pride in their ability to tackle the problem, and fight the fire. These are good skills, but they shouldn't be a product of our inability to address these issues before they become a problem.

This chapter is dedicated to learning how to create that "take-charge" approach to getting things done, not so much for the issues at hand, but for the tasks that need to be addressed in order to achieve your goals. Unless you find ways to create the same kind of urgency to make things happen and execute important tasks—be more proactive—the perceived urgencies will dominate your schedule, and the tasks that would contribute to your goals will consistently get overlooked.

Proactive behavior is defined as our ability to take charge, to take initiative; to create, from within, that sense of urgency to get started on important tasks. Regardless of the *need* to do something, we make it a priority by taking responsibility for our actions and putting it into our daily schedules. Although acting on all of our tasks simultaneously isn't possible, making the effort to prioritize the list and act on our priorities is possible and our responsibility.

Unfortunately, many people do not act on priorities on their terms, proactively. As a result, they are left with a "hot" item, and it then gets dealt with as a crisis or a lost opportunity. In life, this could mean that top priorities never get addressed, and we fail to experience life to its fullest—overlooking much of life's potential.

You prevent crises, you add value to your life, and you are acting responsibly when you take action by choice, on your terms, instead of being driven by external events.

Creating the Urgency

Proactive people get started on projects before they are due; they plan their day; they begin their tax preparation in February; they go to the dentist periodically as a preventative health measure; they work on Friday's deadline days before the panic would normally set in. Proactive people are interested in finding out more about themselves and their potential before circumstances in life require them to.

For example, in seminars I like to ask people, "How many of you would like to learn to play the piano?" About half the room will raise their hands. I'll then single someone out and ask, "Is it urgent that you learn to play the piano in the next three months?" They'll admit that it is not urgent.

I'll then ask, "If your manager said that in three months there would be a position opening here at XYZ corporation that would have some new responsibilities, a twenty percent pay increase, a nicer office, and better vacation package . . . and they really feel that you are perfect for the job . . . but they need someone who can play the piano, would you find a way to learn in the next twelve weeks?"

The person is usually laughing at this point and says yes she will—"In fact, I'm leaving now for my first lesson!" In other words, an external influence (the manager) has placed an urgency on the priority employees had for playing the piano. When a time frame is placed around the priority, they are moved to action: signing up for lessons, scheduling practicing, turning off the television, rearranging the social calendar until the job gets done.

On the other hand, people admit that if the manager never made the offer, it is possible that the dream of playing the piano would drift and possibly never happen. It would always be a great idea, a "want," but there would not be any real need to get it done anytime soon. With a lack of commitment, it will remain unaddressed. With our limited time lines, it is absolutely critical that we develop the ability to create the need ourselves. We must learn to get off our butts and make things happen in our lives independent of what is happening around us.

I have worked with thousands of people on productivity issues and have always been fascinated with the obstacles they face. After watching how they manage their time and the way they plan their day, it is easy to see that most of the stress and "fires" that arise during the day are self-imposed. As deadlines approach, people complain about not having enough time to prepare for meetings, rehearse presentations, or write a report. They point to meeting these deadlines as being a source of stress in their lives. Yet these are often calendared tasks whose deadlines were set well in advance but that were not attacked until they have become crises. This can become habitual, and over time people feel that "that's the way things are around here: We manage by crisis; we put out a lot of fires; we work in a very stressful environment."

The bad habits snowball and become everybody's problem as self-esteem issues and productivity are affected. Actually, with a little discipline on the part of the individual, many problems are preventable.

A Day in the Life

I remember visiting a client at his office in Malibu, California. It was a beautiful building nestled neatly in Las Virgenes Canyon. As I waited for my client to arrive, I marveled at the view of the mountains and the Pacific Ocean. I was glad to have such a view because Bill was already twenty minutes late for the nine o'clock meeting.

Finally, his assistant entered the room and said that Bill was here and I could wait for him in his office. She led me down the hall, and I waited again in his office while he presumably pulled a few things together for the meeting.

I observed the pictures of his family, his golf plaques, read his diplomas, and felt that I knew more about him now that most of his neighbors. As his cherubic children smiled their toothless smiles at me (and strangely seemed to be looking at me), I wondered if his kids knew that "sometimes Daddy is late for work; sometimes Daddy doesn't do his homework; sometimes Daddy doesn't clean his room at the office; Daddy might have missed the bus this morning." I had actually considered tidying up a bit just to stay busy, but figured if Bill walked in as I was cleaning his office, it might look a little strange.

Bill finally arrived like a tornado. He said, "Hi, Ken, sorry I'm late, but it has just been one of those mornings!"

I laughed and said something dumb like, "That's okay, sitting here relaxing has been great . . . just relaxing in this chair . . . here, with the pictures . . . no problem."

He dropped into his chair and unloaded his armload of paperwork and a steaming cup of coffee. He began with a little story of his morning.

"I was ready to leave for work and my wife reminded me that it was trash day. So I had to grab a few things from inside the house and shuttle trash cans from the garage to the curb in a panic so that the truck wouldn't leave the neighborhood without our stuff.

"Then I get in the car and and as I pull away from the house the bright orange "empty" light comes on, which means I have about ten miles to go before I'm walking. As I make my way to the gas station I realize I have about three dollars in my wallet, and need to find an ATM machine for some quick cash. By the time I got all of my morning crises out of the way, I was already twenty minutes late. Sorry, Ken."

We did finally get down to business and my time was eventually well spent.

I have had many days like Bill's. We are all human, and sometimes a few of life's little problems surround us first thing in the morning and, unfortunately, it can affect our mind-set for the rest of the day. Because of a few "fires to fight" at the house, we feel behind and as if we are playing "catch-up" all day at the office. The interesting thing about Bill's morning is that all of his problems were preventable.

Every Wednesday is trash day. He drives the same car every day, and the gas tank is his responsibility. He uses his wallet and spends his money.

Having no sense of urgency or anticipation as well as a lack of planning brought about all of his problems. Proactive behavior prior to the problems would have made his day a little easier.

- If he was proactive on Tuesday and factored into his plan taking out the trash, it would have been one less problem for him Wednesday morning.
- As the gas gauge began showing "medium" and then "low," he could have done something about it on his terms when it was only a priority, rather than when it was a bigger inconvenience and urgency.
- As the money slowly disappeared in his wallet, he could have resolved the problem when it was more convenient rather than when it was absolutely necessary.

If we don't *act* on important events when we should, we are forced to *react* to them when we have to. Many crises can be prevented by

- better planning
- clearer prioritization
- visualizing what our future has in store so we can act now

Any one of the aforementioned ideas (or all three together) will put you in the driver's seat and in better control of your life.

Reactive Behavior

Reactive behavior can be defined as getting work done because there is an external urgency or accountability forcing us to take action—not because we choose to or decide it is the best time. A reactive person floats along waiting for things to happen, and then will respond. Reactive people are the chameleons of the world, always adjusting themselves to what is going on around them. They tend to blame external circumstances: the economy, the weather, their astrological sign, for their status in life. Their lives and their thoughts seem to be at the mercy of the world around them.

Reactive people believe that they are like tea bags: They never really know how good they are until they get in a little hot water.

When a problem arises, the reactive person is forced to scramble and work under stress. If things are left unaddressed or put off, they usually come back to haunt us in the form of a small crisis or at best, an inconvenience. If we aren't proactive and assertive, we end up reactive and victimized.

Reactive people go to the gas station when the needle reads empty—when they are forced to rather than when they choose to; they go to the dentist when there is pain; they do their taxes under the April crunch. A reactive person believes strongly in his or her ability to put out fires as they occur and squeak by getting through any set of circumstances. The problem is that reactive people spend so much time responding to problems today, they rarely see themselves as having time or the option to get ahead of the game and plant seeds and invest in their future. They develop, by default, only average abilities because they never find the time to do things for themselves that will serve them in tapping their potential. Their vision is often limited to wondering about the future versus doing something about it.

Tapping your potential is a proactive process.

You may not have a great need or a deadline to improve your speaking skills, but you do it anyway. There may not be a deadline for you this month to understand more about your retirement planning, your 401K plan, or reading the book about business development, but you start on the activity before it becomes a great need. Steven Covey, author of *The Seven Habits of Highly Effective People*, suggests you "dig the well before you are thirsty." By reading my book, you have demonstrated a curiosity in self-improvement presumably without someone standing over you forcing you to do so. You are acting proactively.

Peace of Mind

There are two different kinds of gratification when being proactive or reactive. The former is clearly rooted in satisfaction and composure; the latter is more a product of getting away with something and sneaking under the wire.

Proactive people, although they experience some short-term, self-imposed urgency, experience long-term, self-made feelings of self-worth and a coolness and collectedness about having their "ducks in a row." With the many things we try to manage in our lives, the only way we ever seem to get in control of these multiple priorities is through proactively taking charge.

Reactive people, although they endure some short-term, self-imposed relaxation and free spiritedness, experience long-term, self-made feelings of stress, disorder, and psychological turmoil. I meet hundreds of people every month whose number-one complaint in the office and at home is the constant number of "surprises" and "fires" that distract from their priorities. There are temporary good feelings of "winging it" and slipping by, but that short-term pleasure is usually accounted for later in the periodic pain they feel in having yet another issue to face.

Part of the discovery process in tapping your potential is to understand that there are many elements about your behavior and performance that are within your control, such as changing your behavior (belief systems, attitude, self-esteem) so it is constructive and inspires feelings of control and empowerment. Proactive behavior will create a life you want. Reactive behavior will create feelings of being controlled by external events and lower your expectations for what you feel you can achieve in life.

Think about how you feel when

- You become the "backseat" driver.
- There's a delay in airline travel.
- Meetings run overtime.
- There are unexpected (or even expected) traffic jams.
- You feel you are falling behind.

Compare those feelings to the kind you experience when

- Bills are paid before penalty dates.
- Deadlines are met.
- Your day is well planned.
- You are ahead of the game.

You only can experience the latter when you proactively attempt to get control of your life. You experience a peace of mind and a sense of balance difficult to acquire when feeling out of control. Your behavior and decisions will determine whether or not you can stay in control and have an impact on the future.

When you are sincerely trying to earn the money you feel you deserve, trying to "break into the business," trying to achieve a level of performance in sports, the only way to get started is by being proactive. When you attempt to make it happen, you prepare yourself mentally for the learning process. And when you are prepared mentally, the body will follow. You will wake up motivated, require less sleep, and observe consciously or subconsciously the many resources you need. You are in the driver's seat in your life, not in the back seat. You make decisions today so you can look forward to results in the future.

You shorten the cycle in tapping your potential when you are proactive.

Be a Thermostat

How is your immediate environment? Is it too hot or too cold? Drafty or too stuffy? Is the music too loud or too low? Is the room too brightly or dimly

> Dost thou love life? Then do not squander time; for that is the stuff life is made of.
> BENJAMIN FRANKLIN

lit? Whatever the status, do you wish it were different?

Drawing from our proactive definition, proactive people will adjust the heat or air conditioning; adjust the lighting; open or close the window; adjust the volume control. They get involved in changing their environment or set of circumstances; or if that is not entirely possible, they will move to a more satisfying environment.

Reactive people in this situation will complain about the environment and wish that things were different; they'll live with the sweat or the chill, or the eyestrain in the poorly lit room. It's like the person who blames their weight problem on the fact that their company provides doughnuts in the lunchroom everyday; or the career criminal who believes that the real problem is the overzealous legal system. It never crossed their minds that their problems are self-imposed and "fixable," not thrown at them.

Proactive people take responsibility for living in a comfortable environment—they "adjust the heat." Reactive people, instead, complain about their environment but do nothing about it. The former approach is responsible, the latter is irresponsible as it tries to pass the blame onto someone or something else.

A good analogy for the distinction between proactive and reactive behavior is the difference between a thermometer and a thermostat.

A thermometer reflects its environment, whereas a thermostat controls its environment. One is reactive (thermometer), the other is proactive (thermostat). If we behave like thermometers, we run the risk of responding to what others want; if we behave like thermostats, we gain the advantage of achieving what we want by taking some action. Have you considered creating a change in your life rather than just wishing that it were different?

Proactive behavior places the power to change in your hands.

Action Items

- Take something in life that is a priority and make it more urgent by proactively calendaring it in your day planner.
- Visualize an entire week or month to better prepare for deadlines today before they become "fires."
- Block out time for yourself to do important things.

SELF-TALK

Faith is the force of life.
LEO TOLSTOY

Part of staying motivated and not letting your enthusiasm
wane is tied to your ability to coach yourself into getting
desired results. Can you stay motivated when things seem to be
going wrong? Can you stay motivated even when things are
going well, but you are growing comfortable? How do you literally coach and counsel yourself into persistence and determination? Can you get from others, or from within, some positive
reinforcement? These conversations you have with yourself can
make the difference between quitting and pressing on.

Your Internal Coach:
Cheerleaders or Hecklers?

The voice you hear when you talk to yourself can be described as
that of a cheerleader or a heckler. It either accents the good or
points out the bad. The "self-comments" you make can be
encouraging or self-defeating. The voices you hear are significant
because they are constantly giving you feedback and making comments which will affect your behavior. The good news is you
decide who sits at the helm of your internal intercom system.

Cheerleaders say "go, go, go." They smile and encourage.
Cheerleaders inspire and cultivate a winning mentality. Even

when the score looks grim, they never leave the sidelines. They help the player maintain confidence in the face of disappointment; they avoid focusing on the reasons why they may lose,

> For they can conquer who believe they can.
>
> JOHN DRYDEN

but instead focus on the possibility of winning. The fans and the cheerleaders play a significant role in fostering necessary team spirit.

Hecklers say "no, no, no." They frown and discourage. Hecklers point out the futility in making the effort and slim chances for success. Your positive attitude can be gradually eroded by these negative vibes and criticism. Hecklers play a dangerous role by deflating your optimism and make failure more likely by robbing you of self-esteem and motivation.

A few months ago I played golf with some friends. I have only been playing a for a short while so I still face many challenges with the game. Once I got comfortable with the plaid pants and funny hat, I began having some fun. What's more, you meet so many nice people while cutting across fairways looking for your little white ball.

All members of our party were on the green. I remember thinking, "If I can sink this putt, I would be setting several personal golf records: par for the hole, winning the hole, using the same ball the entire time, and not having to excuse myself into the woods to find where, exactly, the little bugger landed." No pressure.

I was excited to be on the green in two strokes. So excited, in fact, that I executed a major golf faux pas: running with my putter through a sand trap laughing and yelling, "I can't believe this is happening!" So after I was told to rake my footsteps out of the sand trap, I was allowed to return to the game—a little embarrassed, but still focused.

I was farthest from the cup so I had to putt first. I asked, "If I make this, I'll win the hole, right?"

The rest of the group was quick to point out that a fifteen-foot putt was a challenge at any level of experience, and not to feel bad if it took three additional strokes.

But because I was still caught up in the moment of doing so well, I announced, "Oh, I can make this putt, no problemmo." And I sank the putt.

I attribute this to a little ignorance: I didn't know it was a tough putt; I also used a proper "cheerleader" mentality of encouragement; and because I was clearly more focused on the reward of making the putt, and not the consequences of what would happen if I didn't, I was at ease and followed through. Life is a lot like the game of golf.

Talk to Yourself

Cheerleaders are our support group, hecklers are the enemy, and we will invariably experience both influences. At the office, at home, and in social circles we'll find one of these two groups. We need to be wary of letting the hecklers affect our outlook or behavior. The negative influence changes our vantage point of every problem (or opportunity) we face; (the heckler sees it as a problem; the cheerleader sees it as an opportunity).

This element in the success formula gives you the confidence to tap your potential through trial and error; assuming you will experience some of the common vicissitudes in successes and failures, the right attitude will help you feel confident at the beginning of our quest, optimistic in the middle, and gratified at the end. Positive self-talk gives us the self-assurance to make it work; it strengthens your self-image, and will gather momentum over time.

Shad Helmstedder, in his best-selling book *What to Say When You Talk to Yourself*, describes many different forms of self-talk and positive reinforcement. There is

- silent self-talk (conscious or unconscious internal dialogue)
- self-speak (powerful words and sound bytes that influence)
- self-conversation (the discussions you have with yourself aloud that motivate or appease)
- self-write (working through challenges and coaching oneself through the *written* word)

All are very effective and have been used over the years as a way to ward off negative thoughts and support the positive. Periodically, we all need this type of therapy to offset the barrage of negativity we experience every day. It offers a system of checks and balances to mitigate the doubt and anxiety we may have about doing what we want in life.

Choosing Constructive Comments

For whatever reason, it seems to be a typically human tendency to focus on obstacles and not opportunity; to consistently recall reasons why we may fail than to inventory the reasons why we may succeed. Much like slouching can become a habit of poor posture, we must reposture our thinking through consciously and mentally throwing our shoulders back and introspectively examining the reasons why we *can* make it.

For example, we are quick to say

- Everything I eat goes straight to my waist.
- My desk is always a mess.
- I never have enough time.
- I've never been a good speller.
- I need to get motivated.

And we hesitate to say

- Success is in my blood.
- I really work well with people.
- I have a great memory.
- If they can do it, I can do it.
- Life is a great adventure.

We not only fail to mention these things to ourselves in the form of a "self-speak," we fail to even think it in the privacy of our own minds. This subconscious oversight becomes chronic, and over time we not only live without "cheerleaders" in our lives, we never hear them inside our heads. This creates a hesitancy in trying new things, diminishes our self-esteem, tarnishes our self-image, and lowers our ceiling of expectation, making an endeavor like tapping our potential seem impractical. Take some time to inventory and tally your strengths and best qualities; you owe it to yourself.

Cheerleaders help us see the world with a can-do mentality. We understand that attitude doesn't solve the problem per se, but the cheerleader mentality empowers us to work in every situation more effectively. With the positive self-talk in place, we have more energy, a positive outlook, and create a frame of mind that is conducive to doing well. Unfortunately, people who heckle themselves out of trying to improve their lives never take chances, avoid any and all perceived risk, and therefore may never tap their potential, missing out on some great experiences in life.

Do you remember your first attempt at public speaking? Refer to your belief card-file system under *P* for Public speaking. What does it read? What thoughts and emotions come to mind? Are they good or bad? Most people remember butterflies, the jitters, sweaty palms, and a pounding heart. (Professional speakers still feel these emotions—the key is to put the nervous energy into the presentation.) If you had that kind of experience, do you coach yourself into doing it better next time (cheerleader), or do you allow the heckler to point out why you should stay seated and not risk looking like a complete fool? The good news is you decide who gets your mental microphone as the commentator for the next event—it is a simple choice that you make. For every heckler you hear, there is also a flip side to the argument, with a more encouraging philosophy.

The Flip Side of Challenge

Every interpretation of life's events has two sides. Things can be perceived as either good or bad, success or failure, positive or negative. It may be a thin slice of ham, but there are nonetheless two sides, and you are responsible for choosing the side you see.

Tapping your potential involves focusing on the good side, on the cheerleader's commentary.

In the Chinese language, when the written character for crisis or danger is used, there is another character written beside it—the character that represents opportunity. In the Chinese culture, for every difficult situation you face, for every perceived crisis, there is a flip side: You have simultaneously been presented with an opportunity—an opportunity to change, adapt, grow, learn, and experience.

After having lived through several local crises in Los Angeles, I have noticed that local residents have become quite accustomed to focusing on the flip-side of crisis called opportunity. The riots in May, 1992, forced members of the community to focus on the "rebuild LA" projects. The damage had

> Twixt the optimist and pessimist
> The differences is droll:
> The optimist sees the doughnut
> But the pessimist sees the hole.
> McLANDBURGH WILSON

been done. We could focus on all of the damage and the loss, or see how we could somehow learn from the experience, put people to work, and form business opportunities for those working and living in Los Angeles. Members of the community realized that they would not make the situation any better by focusing on the negative. We all had to focus on the flip side to see what new opportunities we had.

On January 17, 1994, I was thrown out of bed by a 6.7 earthquake, the largest single disaster in U.S. history. I remember thinking, "Mondays are bad enough, and now this." People felt the earthquake from Las Vegas to San Diego. My home is fifteen miles from the epicenter. After picking up what was thrown on the floor from our refrigerators, the broken dishes, the spilled books from shelves, the fallen pictures, and broken sliding-glass doors, we all had to find out what was in it for us as a community. There was a lot of damage (twenty billion dollars, in fact) that needed repair, and a lot of morale problems that needed fixing as well.

It takes a unique mentality to shrug off yet another natural disaster and take the stress and anxiety and invest it in doing all that can be done to make living in Los Angeles less dangerous

> The optimist proclaims that we live in the best of all possible worlds; and the pessimist fears this is true.
>
> JAMES BRANCH CABELL

and more enjoyable. Many chose to see the fires, floods, riots, mud slides, earthquakes (have I missed anything?) as the price you pay for living in a state with near-perfect weather nine months out of the year and not having to deal with the other expenses and responsibilities that states with four seasons must face. It is simply viewed as a fair and expected trade-off. Los Angeles does have four seasons: fires, floods, mud slides, and earthquakes—home sweet home.

On the business side, during these times of crisis, while some companies pulled back, many companies increased their exposure to organizations and people. They tied their product to a solution to getting things back to normal. Contributions to good causes were made, people fed and housed the newly homeless, hotel rooms were donated to the cause, not to mention the money made by T-shirt promoters, baseball-hat memorabilia, and, "quake sales."

With the amount of repair on freeways and buildings, many of our unemployed could look forward to months of productive work. The increased work force would bring more tax revenues to the city and county of Los Angeles. We learned a lot about the safety of bridges, tunnels, and freeway overpasses that can be applied to future construction. People in the community pulled together and once again overcame adversity.

Earthquakes are not good; riots are not pleasant events. The only thing we can do in those predicaments is be as resourceful as we can to make the best of it. The basic lesson applies to the CEO, the housewife, the child, the athlete, to anyone. When focusing on the opportunity, we gear up to reap something valuable from the experience; it takes our attention away from the recent shortcoming and reinvests the frustration and the energy into making the experience somehow constructive.

> That which does not kill me makes me stronger.
> FREDERICK WILHELM NEITZCHE

Because we do not live in Disneyland, and because the rest of the world doesn't take a personal interest in our well-being, we will be faced with many challenges. The flip side, the bright side, of every situation in life must become our primary concern. It will limit the time we dwell on a problem, and get us a head start on finding a solution.

The flip side:

- Lemons into lemonade
- The glass half-empty now is half full
- Partly cloudy turned partly sunny
- Stumbling blocks turn to stepping stones
- Failure is a valuable lesson
- Crisis is opportunity

W. Clement Stone and Napoleon Hill in their classic book *Success Through a Positive Mental Attitude* remind us that for every perceived negative experience, a seed of equivalent benefit is planted. In other words, there is a silver lining to every challenge you face. And any expert in the field of human development will tell you that people's perception of their ability to accomplish a

---

There's a Pony Around Here Somewhere

Two brothers were running through a field. They stumbled across a barn. In their excitement, they ran inside and found nothing but a pile of horse manure. One brother decided to leave. The remaining brother shouted, "Hold on! There's gotta be a pony around here somewhere!"

Whatever the situation, *find the pony.*

respectable objective, or a worthy goal, is a major factor in whether or not they'll give up early and quit or stick with it and see it fully realized. Perception will create feelings; feelings will create an attitude; attitude leads to a cheerleader or heckler mentality, which ultimately affects your behavior. Therefore, how you interpret life's experiences will have an impact on your behavior. Be sure the interpretation is conducive to tapping potential.

Tapping your potential is only made possible if you can persevere; and perseverance is affected by your perception.

Action Items

- Any time you doubt yourself and a heckler begins to comment, stop and replace the negative thinking with more positive thinking.
- Consciously practice better self-talk or self-speak to realign your thinking into the proper groove.
- Think of a recent setback in your life, and then consider the possible good that came of it; the opportunity will present itself to you.

GREAT EXPECTATIONS

I am giddy, expectation whirls me 'round.
The imaginary relish is so sweet
That it enchants my sense.

WILLIAM SHAKESPEARE

One very important element in our belief system is how well we think we can do, how much we think we can succeed, and how far we think we can carry our potential. The number of books we can write, the number of languages we can speak, the number of customers we can have, and the amount of money we can earn are all tied to our self-expectancy. If we believe that "we don't always get what we want in life, but we almost always get what we expect," it is our responsibility to set high expectations.

To the degree that you raise your expectations about your performance, you will tap your potential.

Self-Expectancy

You shouldn't think of your potential as being "out" there somewhere, but as being "up" there somewhere. How high can you climb the ladder, to what heights can you aspire, how much can you grow as a person? And wherever you decide to set that marker, just like an athlete raising the high bar, you must believe you are capable of clearing that mark. Your achievement expectations are not influenced by factual projections as much as they are determined by perception and belief.

If I asked a roomful of people how many languages they could learn to speak, one person may say three, the next two, and the next may say seven. All of the answers are based on expectations given their aptitude and how much time they are willing to invest in the project. One liberating thought to consider when raising our expectations is that the world is "our oyster" and our very own blank check. We have complete freedom to go as far as we want and do as well as we want—but that potential will be influenced by our self-expectancy.

This potential will be determined by a "glass ceiling" you have placed on your performance. It is a glass ceiling because it does exist although you cannot see it. You assume it is there and avoid bumping your head on it by rising too quickly, so you play it safe anywhere below the ceiling.

These beliefs about your potential are not always expressed, but they're implied through your decisions; they are subconscious beliefs you hold because of past conditioning, self-esteem issues, and what you may have filed away in your belief card-file system. For example, you will apply for a job or you won't because of the number of responsibilities you think you can handle. Or perhaps you don't see yourself (a belief about who you are) earning a higher salary. If the ceiling is lower than the possible opportunity, you will never make the attempt. Remember, be sure that what you believe about yourself is constructive and will raise your ceiling of expectation and not lower it. You must hold beliefs that give you the motivation and self-esteem to feel worthy of receiving what you want in life.

Self-Esteem

Self-esteem is much more than just feeling good or being happy or not being depressed. Nathaniel Branden, considered to be the father of the self-esteem movement, and author of *The Psychology of Self-Esteem* and *The Power of Self-Esteem*, defines self-esteem as "confidence in our ability to think and cope with the challenges in life" and "confidence in our right to be happy, the feeling of being worthy, deserving, and entitled to assert our needs and wants to enjoy the fruits of our efforts." Naturally, the confidence aspect will serve us well because without it, we won't show up for auditions, we won't pursue the goal, we won't apply for the job, and we won't ask for the promotion. Self-esteem means we feel we have the necessary resources to meet the challenges of life and deal with any problems we may face.

I meet people all the time in seminars that actually question whether or not they could cope with achieving their goals. They experience a false sense of humility or guilt in getting what they want; for example, "Why should I do so well? Why should I have the money? Why should I get to play golf during the week?" and they therefore sabotage their efforts in order to not have to deal with the "pain."

Or people actually fear getting what they want because they worry about creating a void: What will they then have to hope and wish for? Another fear is getting what they want and not having it be everything they dreamed about. They make more money and then ask, "Is that it? I thought this was supposed to feel a lot better." So in order to prevent the disappointment in finding their dream is not as good as it looks on TV, they don't do anything about it and prefer to live with the fantasy.

If you agree with Branden's definition, then you agree that you have a right to be happy; you have a right to plant the seeds and reap the harvest; you should feel comfortable demonstrating your talents and utilizing your resources to get what you want; and if that is to help others, sculpt, have a great family, or work out of your home, then you are entitled to that. But you must esteem yourself to the point that those dreams actually become options.

- Self-esteem gives you the confidence and the energy to want to tap your potential. Self-esteem gives you the energy to want to get out of bed in the morning. When depression and feelings of uselessness or helplessness take over, you feel like you are dragging a piano around all day and are ineffectual in your ability to do much good for yourself.

- Self-esteem *provides* you with enthusiasm, which helps you deal with the occasional failure and recover more quickly from small setbacks. It provides the confidence to take chances, stick your neck out on occasion, and take on projects unfamiliar or challenging to you.
- Self-esteem *cultivates* working relationships. With good self-esteem you don't feel threatened by others' great ideas and successes. It gives you the self-assuredness to add your two cents and contribute to discussions. All of the byproducts of self-esteem manifest themselves in ways that are recognized by others and make you a pleasant and productive human being in the course of your daily relations.

Ken Blanchard, in his best-selling book *The One-Minute Manager*, does a wonderful job of explaining the importance of self-esteem. He believes that how we feel about ourselves actually shows through in the work that we produce. He said that "people who feel good about themselves produce good results." And self-esteem is such a critical factor in working environments that occasionally we should "Help people reach their full potential. Catch them doing something right—and let them know about it." It doesn't cost anything, and a compliment and recognition will go a long way in fostering team spirit.

Kids at Heart

I believe that somewhere along the line adults have forgotten that they are still very much kids at heart. There are emotions that are better suppressed as adults, but the feelings are experienced nonetheless. We are careful to treat children appropriately, and reckless at times in our treatment of one another.

If your three-year-old niece takes a piece of paper and a crayon and draws a series of concentric circles that resemble a human face, then hands it to you and says, "Look! there's a picture of you!" how do you react?

Naturally, you respond, "Great! That's beautiful! Go make another one!" You'd never say, "Close, but no cigar. That's not what I look like. Try using a better pen." We don't want to discourage the child and rob her of her self-esteem; we want her to feel good about trying new things. If she feels that by taking a chance, her self-worth is threatened, she'll never make the attempt.

> All you need in this life is ignorance and confidence, and then success is sure.
> MARK TWAIN

And that is exactly what you must keep in mind when you hear the heckler from the previous chapter whispering in your ear. If you accept his negative comments it will impact your future behavior and attempts at success. You must "feed" your own self-esteem, give yourself a pat on the back, and take special note of your achievements if you want to tap your potential. Treat yourself like you'd treat a child—with a great deal of understanding, good solid support, and be firm but constructive in the area of discipline.

In order to help individuals, at home or in the workplace, maximize their potential, you must always cultivate feelings of self-worth and self-esteem. We are kids at heart because we love to be recognized for a job well done, and we can't help but feel a little empty when we do a great job and it goes completely overlooked. In fact, Earl Nightingale, the great peak-performance writer and lecturer said that recognition is one of the most important human needs. Apply your sincere compliments liberally over other deserving people.

In terms of coaching others and empowering them to tap their potential, treat people as successes-in-the-making. Goethe said it best when he suggested, "If you treat an individual as he is, he will remain as he is; but if you treat him as if he were what he ought to be and could be, he will become what he ought to be and could be." You must feed and fertilize the self-esteem within the individual.

Without self-esteem you won't have the desire to tap your potential; with high self-esteem you will feel that living your potential is entirely possible.

You Exist in Your Imagination

How do you see yourself? Where do you see yourself? Do you have a healthy self-image? If you refer back to your belief card-file system, and look under the card entitled Me, what does it say? If it says, "I'm a terrible speller," you misspell the words and attribute it to your inability to spell. People who behave as if they are poor spellers rarely look up the word in the dictionary and write it five times to ensure they get it right the next time—that wouldn't be "like them." They use the spell check on the computer or have their assistant revise it for them. Because they see themselves that way, the behavior will remain that way. Whichever aspect you focus on when

> People rarely exceed their own self-image.
> BRIAN TRACEY

evaluating your self-image, you can identify a behavior pattern that exists in support of that belief about who you are.

If I gave you an incentive of $1,000 for an "A" on a twenty-five-word spelling test, would you study any harder or apply yourself more? Of course you would. And because you worked a little harder, you'll do much better. In other words, you have the potential to be a good speller, you simply believe it to be otherwise—therefore leaving great potential laying dormant.

"A" students do what it takes to master the material. They have always worked hard and received good results. Because they think of themselves and see themselves as winners, they practice and apply themselves like winners. The self-image manifests itself through achieved results.

Arnold Schwarzenegger, a man I've always admired and wanted to meet, always envisioned himself as a champion. His vision of success was so great, it brought him to the United States from Austria when he was only twenty. His dreams of being a world-class bodybuilder and champion became fully realized. His friends today remember his consistently optimistic attitude and focus.

His dream of owning property is Southern California was so great that he went to evening classes at Santa Monica City Community College to learn more about real estate. He eventually bought the building in which he lived in Santa Monica, and was on his way. Through trial and error and consistently working at being the best, he currently owns an enormous amount of real estate in Los Angeles.

> Imagination is more important than knowledge.
>
> ALBERT EINSTEIN

Schwarzenegger's desire to be an actor and break into show business was so great he took speech lessons to refine his Austrian accent. He struggled to get an agent but was repeatedly turned away. Perhaps that's where the idea of "I'll be back" originated. He networked every day with anyone who could put him on film—in any role. He carefully planned his days and set his sights on Hollywood.

You may remember him in the not-so-smashing success *Hercules in New York*. They actually had his voice dubbed because of his accent. He took his knocks to get his start, but he always saw himself as a million-dollar actor who had simply not been given his chance.

After the documentary *Pumping Iron* was released, more people grew to understand him and the sport, and he positioned himself wisely as the man who worked hard and ultimately won championships. That film was marketed in such a way that it opened other doors of opportunity.

The rest of the Schwarzenegger story is well known. His movies have consistently been top box-office draws. Because he took the time to learn about producing, directing, marketing, and the royalties and merchandising side of the business, he played a part in all of those capacities and has made himself one of the wealthiest men in Hollywood. Not bad for a kid who didn't learn to speak English fluently until age twenty-one.

(I did finally meet Arnold Schwarzenegger at his restaurant,

Schatzi, in Venice, California. It cost me about $500 in lunches until he finally showed up one day, but it was well worth it.)

You've got to dream big, believe big, and persevere big if you want to discover your potential.

In Your Wildest Dreams

Reverend Robert Schuller, author of many books including *Tough Times Never Last, But Tough People Do!*, asks an amusing and thought-provoking question in his lectures: "What would you attempt to do if you knew you couldn't fail?" Be realistic. If being an astronaut is out of the question, don't write it down. Within your range of possibilities, what would you do and what could you be doing now if you knew you couldn't fail?

Close the book and think about it for a second . . .

Now . . . do you have any real, legitimate, concrete reasons why that is not attainable?

And for the people that have the things or do the things you want, are they so much different than you in so many ways that you feel inferior? What would you have to do in order to get there? I am sure there is a strategy you could put to paper and pursue that would put you closer to your dream. Planning for the future will be discussed later; for now, the purpose of including Schuller's question is to experiment with the imagination and recognize that your only limitations are your expectations.

The other question that helps us look at the options we have and our world of opportunity comes from Alan Lakein in his book *How to Get Control of Your Time and Your Life.* "What's the worst thing that would happen if . . . ?" Think about things you've been tempted to try but haven't, about a chance you've been meaning to take but have been shy or afraid; the phone call you've almost made but presupposed the answer. Elimenate some uneccessary anxiety by asking Lakein's question. "What's the worst thing that would happen if I did (fill in the blank) and it didn't work out? If you can live with the consequences (and usually they are far less significant than you imagine), then you really have nothing to lose.

What's the worst thing that would happen if you applied for a job and didn't get it? What's the worst thing that would happen if you called a high-level person in an organization and asked for business? What's the worst thing that would happen if you auditioned for a part in a play and it didn't work out? If you can live with the worst-case scenario, take the chance. You wouldn't have what you now don't have anyway. At times you must s-t-r-e-t-c-h. If you knew you could succeed, and it would make you a better person, give it a go. Successful people are those who take bigger steps, longer strides, ask bigger questions and make bigger demands of life without the fear of failure.

Within reason, the worst-case-scenario question can be a very effective motivator to try new things—and sometimes it is those new little things that can alter the course of a person's life for the better; it is extremely liberating and eliminates the very "mental blocks" that have stood between you and your goals.

Shift the Focus

You sometimes become so focused on what may happen if things don't go according to plan that in your mind it becomes a major problem and it burdens you to the point where picking up the phone or writing a letter seems at best futile. People who are able to tap their potential have done so by taking some perceived chances and obvious risks. They live with the confidence of being able to live productive, happy lives despite the outcome—they knew they would be okay as people even though the results may not have been the greatest. And when you all reach the end of your timeline one day, you will never have regrets or remorse for not trying things when you had the chance. Try shifting the focus from the pain of possible failure to the pleasure of potential success.

Estimating Your Potential

Think about something you are very good at doing. Is it playing a musical instrument, competing in a sport, speaking eloquently, writing, singing . . . ? How much potential do you have in that area? You probably have much more than you think, and you will never know for sure until you begin asking and demanding of life what you feel you deserve. Start today.

We have on this planet more potential than can be described here or in all the libraries in the world:

We have the power to

- Eliminate crime immediately
- Significantly reduce pollution
- Control population explosions
- Stop all wars and conflict
- Control government spending
- Increase the density of the rain forests
- Save animal species from extinction
- Stop abuse
- Give

It's a long shot, but if we got everyone in the world to cooperate and work—even for a day—toward a specific goal, the results would be mind-boggling. To a lesser degree, if we were able to get the people of the United States to cooperate—even for a day—on one of their many problems—the results would be mind-boggling. If we got the people in our neighborhoods to cooperate—even for a day—on a local problem, the results would be very exciting. We know this works because when people in neighborhoods and communities get together and cooperate to resolve a local problem, it gets resolved! Many of our problems are self-imposed, and many of the solutions are self-administered.

If every person in your state agreed

- Not to assault another person
- To pick up one piece of garbage
- Wear a seat belt today
- To be responsible for children brought into this world
- To shorten their daily shower by sixty seconds
- To lay down their guns
- To do a charitable act

what would be the results? Very, very impressive.

If we took these examples and brought them into the only life we can control—our own—what would be the results? Really exciting—well, at least surprising, gratifying, and maybe even life-changing. If we can't always benefit from collected potentials, we can at least set our expectations high in our lives for the changes we can make for ourselves. If you "cultivate your own garden," to paraphrase Voltaire, you must put yourself in a position to help others in the world around you.

Tapping your potential is made possible by your belief that you have the wherewithal to make it happen.

Action Items

- Consider how far you'd like to take one of your talents.
- In order to help others reach their potential, provide an encouraging word and feed their self-esteem.
- Think of something that you really want in life, and work on making it happen immediately; remember to ask yourself, "What's the worst thing that would happen if . . . ?" If you can live with the possible outcome, then take the chance.

VALUES

A musician must make music,
an artist must paint,
a poet must write, if he is to be
ultimately at peace with himself.

ABRAHAM MASLOW

In order to tap your potential, you must be motivated to pursue something close to your heart. Everyone has passions and interests in their lives, and they should motivate you to the point of wanting to act on them. In other words, people want to create lives for themselves where there will be time and a means for doing what they feel is important. You feel frustrated, stressed, and unfulfilled when what you *do* has nothing to do with what you *value*. You are gratified and feel a sense of peace when you act on your priorities.

An important part of tapping your potential will involve identifying that which you view as a priority in life; it may be a value for financial wellness, intellectual growth, or philanthropy—you must be clear on your "motivators" and then strategize about what you will do with them. Tapping your potential is made possible by identifying your priorities. If you pursue things that are not truly important to you, you will be easily discouraged by the first few setbacks you encounter. You simply won't care about it enough to weather out the challenges.

The Wisdom of Hindsight

The following experiment should be taken seriously—because it will happen to each of us at least once in a lifetime: death. It is the great equalizer, it is an end we all must face, and just thinking about it makes people more philosophical than any other natural occurrence—next to contemplating life. If you could see death on your horizon, what would you do with your time?

I didn't include this in the book to bring people down, only to remind readers of a part of life that makes it interesting: mortality. It is the end of your time line that creates the need to make good use of the beginning and middle. And, unfortunately, most people discover what was really important and how they should have lived their lives after it is too late. Can we benefit vicariously from the wisdom passed on to us by those who have

---

If I Had My Life to Live Over Again

If I had my life to live over again, I'd dare to make more mistakes. I'd relax. I'd limber up. I would be sillier than I have this trip. I would take fewer things seriously. I would take more chances. I would take more trips. I would climb more mountains and swim more rivers. I would eat more ice cream and less beans. I would perhaps have more actual troubles but I'd have fewer imaginary ones.

You see, I'm one of those people who live sensibly and sanely hour after hour, day after day.

Oh, I've had my moments and if I had to do it over again, I'd have more of them. In fact, I'd try to have nothing else. Just moments. One after the other, instead of living so many years ahead of each day.

I've been one of those people who never go anywhere without a thermometer, a hot water bottle, a raincoat, and a parachute.

If I had to do it again, I would travel lighter next time. I would start barefoot earlier in the spring and would stay that way later in the fall. I would go to more dances. I would ride more merry-go-rounds. I would pick more daisies.

NADINE STAIR (Age 85)

reached the rocking chair and express all of the things they "coulda, woulda, and shoulda" done?

Yyour life has tremendous potential. Identifying and addressing yyour values allows you to apply yyour potential in the most rewarding ways.

Without elaborating on the number of possible lost opportunities you could experience, my request is that you take some time and actually visualize yourself much older. What do you wish you did when you had the chance in your twenties, thirties, forties, etc.? Have no regrets.

If your goals and dreams are not value-driven, you will not fully tap your potential. You must know what matters most in your life.

The Stuff of Which Goals Are Made

If you have ever decided to make some changes, been ready to turn over a new leaf for the new year, or been ready to find the "new you" right after your next birthday, you have finally decided to do something about a priority in your life. You may have decided to quit smoking, earn more money, start your own business, or climb the corporate ladder because these goals are tied to areas of great importance: values for health, financial security, or career advancement.

Knowing what your values are is important for three reasons:

- Values are the very foundation upon which your goals are based; when you set a goal, you ask "what do I like to do?" or "what is important to me?"
- Values are the motivating force behind your desire to set goals and tap your potential in the first place. (You picked up this book because you are motivated to improve in certain areas, and are probably addressing the value you have for personal growth.)

- Values give you clarity and direction by helping you determine which goals are most important.

Therefore, you must arrive at a definition for values and how you can identify them.

Values Defined

Values can be defined as everything from top priorities in life to the behavioral characteristics that set our standards of performance. They can be the priorities tied to being a good parent, an active volunteer, or a successful career person. They can also include professional standards or intellectual and spiritual ideals. They prompt us to pursue family activities, vacation time, or to hunt through bookstores and antique shops. They are our subjective assessment of the meaning of life.

A thorough values identification process will include *writing them down*. Get a pen and paper and begin putting some of life's important issues to paper. This enables you to visualize what is important and is a great help in the thought process; each idea on paper will prompt more thinking and discovery.

As you list your values, you may find that some are abstract—it will be difficult to determine specific goals designed to manifest the value. Other values will more readily lend themselves to traditional step-by-step goals. This is the difference between *behavioral* and *actionable* values.

Behavioral Values

The first types of values for discussion will be the ones manifested more by our *behavior* than by the goals we pursue. Although we established that our values are the stuff that dreams and goals are made of, not every value we have can easily be transformed into a goal. A value for financial security is addressed

by a savings plan and investment
objectives, but what goals are set based
on honesty and integrity? Stop lying?
Steal a little less this month than I did
last month? These values may be

Well done is better than
well said.

BEN FRANKLIN

viewed as virtues or good moral qualities. They are very important but not so *actionable* as others.

The following are some examples of behavioral values which
are important but difficult to measure and not easily developed
into goals:

* honesty
* integrity
* positive attitude
* high self-esteem
* respect for others
* being a good listener
* remaining flexible

It could be argued that it is possible to set a goals for being a
better listener: There are books that can be read and seminars
that can be attended, but measuring results can be tricky. How
could you measure that you are a ten percent better listener this
month than last? These are tough to measure but without question must be present, woven into the fabric of our behavior, and
play a critical part in our ability to achieve goals and tap our
potential.

Furthermore, even if you could improve a value called
"respect for others" in two months time, you wouldn't set that
value aside to address others. While you might have a value tied
to personal finances, once you open the IRA, that value may take
a backseat temporarily to address other areas of importance.
Behavioral values such as attitude and honesty are always going to
be part of the process—they can coexist. Honesty doesn't need to
take a backseat to spontaneity; they will work concurrently in
our lives and are not mutually exclusive.

Actionable Values

Actionable values easily lead to more concrete goals that can be broken down into manageable steps. They become the driving force behind actual projects and concrete accomplishments. For example:

- physical fitness
- financial security
- financial independence
- intellectual growth
- family time
- community involvement
- having fun
- political involvement
- education
- professional development
- professional advancement
- better nutritional habits

You can address these types of values by asking, "If these are really important to me, what have I done about them lately? If these are the greatest motivators for me in my life, am I *proactively* addressing a specific objective tied to a value? If intellectual growth is important to me, what am I going to do about it in the next few months?" There is a big difference between just *having* a value and proactively addressing it through goal setting. The latter gets results!

For example:

- A value for intellectual growth could motivate you to go back to school and earn a degree. It could motivate you to read thirty books this year. It could prompt you to visit the local museum and landmarks in your community. You can calendar a value-driven objective. You should demonstrate what is important to you through your actions.

- A value for having fun could motivate you to plan a vacation. It could prompt you to to take dancing or singing lessons. You might even sign up for a local softball league.
- A value for community involvement could motivate you to chair a fund raiser. It could prompt you to organize a "feed-the-homeless" day each month. It could be the reason you want to donate some of your expertise to less-fortunate groups.

Most people can't find a task on their last thirty to-do lists that has anything to do with important issues. There are a whole host of tasks committed to getting through the day, but very few plant seeds for the future. The key to getting actively involved in creating your future is by aligning today's activities with your values and your goals.

You will never tap your potential if your time each day is absorbed by merely getting through the day. You must do something each day that improves your chances for future success.

Regardless of how many values you think you have and can identify now (two or two hundred), the roster that is identified is the "stuff" that goals are made of. Tapping your potential will involve taking an inventory of what makes your life go 'round (and what should make it go 'round) and pursuing those values with greater attention and diligence. A value that doesn't get any attention creates a void in your life and can also be a source of stress due to the frustration of never having time for things that matter.

Once again, the change you are trying to make is to not only *recognize* that some items are important, but to *act* on them through a specific activity or by pursuing a goal.

More examples:

- You value physical fitness, so you want to lose weight, quit smoking, start exercising again.

- You value being organized, so you are now committed to getting the garage organized, putting our finances in order, and redoing the closets.

- You have a value for intellectual growth, so you are now prepared to take an evening course in screenwriting, finish the MBA, or learn to speak French.

All the people I've helped work through this process of identifying values—including myself—feels enthusiastic and a great deal of optimism that they are about to make a change for the better or do something good for themselves. They also experience a peace of mind that a sense of impending balance and control now exists in their lives. They are "pumped up" about the new year's resolution just by writing a few things on paper. It feels good.

The Center of the Wheel

People are often surprised to find that a single value can lead to many different kinds of goals. For example, a value for *generosity* can lead to volunteering at a hospital, running in a fund-raising marathon, or dedicating some time to a local school district. Picture the value at the center of a wheel, and each of the spokes represent the different goals that could be pursued.

The process can also work in reverse. You could pursue the same goal many times over, but the value driving that goal could be different each time. For example, you travel to Maui, Hawaii. Why are you going? The following are possible values motivating you to pursue the objective of traveling to Maui.

- *You love your family*—you travel there twice a year to spend some quality time together.
- *You value being successful in your work*—you travel there twice a year to visit clients, meet with your distributors, attend conferences.

• *You value higher education*—you may be a geology major at a university and have decided to write your thesis on some aspect of the volcanoes. You're in Maui to do the needed research.

Again, one value can lead to many different goals; and a single goal can be a product of many different values. The key is to begin with the important values and let that set the course and direct you toward your goals.

When we can look at a list of our life's priorities, we will feel as if we have our hands on our own personal compass in life. It points us in the proper direction. Once we feel we are headed in the right direction, we need to determine what it is we want to achieve along the way in the form of goal-setting. Values will serve as our navigator; goals become our destination.

The opposite of this will be true too. If we aren't sure what is important or we lack direction, we can't feel that our time has been well spent because we haven't figured out what we should be doing. It is impossible to feel truly gratified by activities that

> Death, so called, is a thing which makes men weep, And yet a third of life is passed in sleep.
> LORD BYRON

don't contribute to our self-worth or add value to our lives. We feel as if we are drifting rather than on track.

Activities that are tied to goals are like a coin deposited in a piggy bank. We are, after all, trying to add value to our lives. If your behavior conflicts with your priorities, that is tantamount to taking money out of the piggy bank. It steals from feelings of self-worth, creating feelings of guilt or low self-esteem.

The key will be to get the behavior (how you are) in line with the value (what is a priority) and then move toward a desired destination (what you want).

In order to tap potential, there must be congruency between behavior and values.

In Marsha Sinetars great book *Do What You Love, the Money Will Follow*, she recommends asking the following questions in an attempt to live out more fully your purpose in life:

- What do I want to have accomplished when I look back at my life in old age?
- How would I have to think, speak, and act in order to bring my *purpose* into being? (What habits would I need to cultivate and what would I have to delete from my present life to live out my true purpose?)

> Things which matter most in life must never be at the mercy of things which matter least.
>
> GOETHE

- What activities—what actual daily choices, attitudes, and concrete accomplishments—would I do if I lived as if my purpose meant something to me?
- How would I live, on a day-to-day basis, if I respected myself, others, and my life's purpose?

Powerful questions. Most people (there's that phrase again) are afraid to consider what changes would have to be made for fear of discovering that what they have been doing has nothing to do (or may even be in conflict) with where they hope to be going. This inventory takes probably thirty minutes and can literally alter the course of your life, as well as make significant changes in daily behavior for the better.

You can never tap your potential for long-term results if the short-term behavior is self defeating.

Is There Overlap?

To illustrate the importance of having behavior and values more closely aligned, note the following example. The objective is to have congruency or conjunction (overlap between our values and behavior) and avoid disjunction (disparity or a gap between how we behave and what we value). See Figure 8.1.

The disparity between behavior and values (disjunction) is where your activities do not support your values and may even

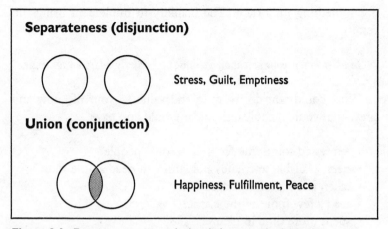

Figure 8.1: Emotions experienced when behavior and values are separate contrasted with emotions experienced when they are congruent.

conflict with them. The union of behavior and values (conjunction) is when a few things on today's to-do list are in line with values and in support of your goals.

For example, you may have a value for being honest. If you find a wallet in the street and decide to return it to its rightful owner, the gratification you experience is worth more than the thrill of keeping the wallet and the money—your behavior is in support of the value. You did the right thing.

If you force yourself to exercise, have the discipline to pass on dessert, and stick to the savings plan, you experience inner peace because your behavior is aligned with what you value. It has been said that inner peace is realizing that what you *are* doing and what you *ought* to be doing is the same thing. You can experience that kind of growth process every day by spending your time wisely.

Some people, due to their inability to do something about the things they want, fail to ever reach their goals. "I've been meaning to do this; as soon as I have time, I'll do that; one day, when the weather gets better, right after my birthday, and this New Year's I'm going to . . ." This is a lazy and ineffective way to preface something important. The inability to implement brings no results.

In order to tap your potential, you must proactively address your values.

What could you do today to add value to your life now and prevent a woulda, coulda, shoulda? Could you have

- expressed some true feelings to some people?
- been available to friends and family in need a little more?
- taken a few more vacations?
- read a few more of the classics
- spent more time in nature?
- taken a few more "risks"?
- planted a garden?

Whatever it is you fear regretting, turn those fears into actions to do something about it today. You can drive yourself into action today because you know in your heart that in the last analysis, they are the things you value most.

Living Tomorrow's Eulogy

If you've attended a funeral, you know the purpose of a eulogy. It literally means "good speech" about a person who has just died. It highlights accomplishments, lists qualities about their character, and notes achievements. It is what we will remember most about the person.

If you had to write your own eulogy, what could you say? If you knew your eulogy would be needed in ten years, what would you begin doing today so you could be proud of the content? If you could eavesdrop on you own funeral, what would you hear? Or what would you like to hear?

The great humorist Will Rogers said we should live our lives so that we wouldn't mind selling the family parrot to the town gossip. Mark Twain suggested, "Let us endeavor so to live that when we die, even the undertaker will be sorry." We all should do things we can be proud of and earn you self-respect. If you throw yourself mentally to the end of your time line, you will discover what you should do today. You must put to paper a strategy to protect time for what you feel is important.

> If you would not be forgotten as soon as you are dead, either write things worth reading, or do things worth writing.
> BENJAMIN FRANKLIN

Values As a Moving Target

Your list of values is dynamic, not static. You will experience a whole host of events in life that will be value-changing experiences, events that may make you reconsider your behavior or change the ranking of the values from the top of the list to the bottom.

Imagine your doctor reports that you have a high cholesterol count. You may be in danger if your diet and sedentary lifestyle continue. The recommendation is a change in eating habits and an introduction to a four-day-a-week exercise program. Physical fitness gets placed at the center of your discretionary time, and time to pursue other activities gets put on the back burner.

Or what if your manager tells you that the organization is changing rapidly, and you will be receiving a promotion that will temporarily involve longer hours and some professional development time. Career values now move up the list taking a higher rank than other values. A promotion will change the priority of the values and have an impact on the daily activities you pursue.

When you take time to write your values, remember that the list is not carved in stone. What seems critically important today can change over time; what may have been a low priority one year soon evolves into a primary concern for you (such as retirement planning); and as you grow, you acquire some values you didn't consider earlier in life (children, spouse, health). You must be aware of top priorities to ensure you are doing the right things.

An important part of tapping your potential will involve successfully juggling the complexity of life's priorities, making the right decisions as to what needs attention, and then acting on it.

Live and Learn

Dr. Robert S. Eliot tells his story in his popular and well-respected book *Is It Worth Dying for?* As one of the most respected cardiologists in the country, he found himself writing constantly, speaking to large groups, and traveling the country—at the same time avoiding other issues (values) that were important, such as family, relaxation, and eating the right foods. He suffered a heart-attack and was forced (or given the opportunity, depending upon how you see it) to rethink his lifestyle and behavior. That is a common event for heart attack patients: Resting in the recovery room thinking about the job, people, diet, or outside events that caused the heart attack—realizing that it may call for a change in priorities. Unfortunately it is often a small tragedy in life that makes people look within to gain some perspective and make changes.

Being a Scrooge

In Charles Dickens' *A Christmas Carol*, we recall seeing Ebenezer Scrooge being shown his behavior at different stages in his life by the Ghost of Christmas Past, the Ghost of Christmas Present, and the Ghost of Christmas to Come. In the final visit to the future, he finds he is unloved, not missed after dying, and, in fact, given a quick, insensitive riddance by all who knew him. When he awakens, his sense of joy and relief upon learning it has all been a dream brings about immediate behavior changes. He is now no longer stingy, but giving; he is no longer unfriendly and hateful, but outgoing and loving. He is motivated to immediately change his behavior because of a vivid experience of what the future may hold if the old behavior continues. In a sense, he is moved, not to second-guess what the future holds for him, but to create it by changing his present behavior:

"Ghost of the future!" he exclaims, "I fear you more than any spectre I have seen. But as I know your purpose is to do me good, and as I hope to live to be another man from what I was, I am prepared to bear you company, and do it with a thankful heart." And later:

"Before I draw nearer to that stone to which you point," says Scrooge, "answer me one question. Are these the shadows of the things that will be or are they shadows of the things that may be, only?" Still the ghost pointed downward to the grave by which it stood.

"Men's courses will foreshadow certain ends, to which, if persevered in, they must lead," says Scrooge. "But if the courses be departed from, the ends will change. Say it is thus with what you show me!" And finally:

"Good spirit," he pursued, as down upon the ground he fell before it, "your nature intercedes for me, and pities me. Assure me that I yet may change these shadows you have shown me, by an altered life!"

Your life may not call for a major rewiring. You're not leading an evil life that lacks humanity or creates misery for others. But most people do discover that they could be better. And perhaps a quick analysis of how you have spent your time would reveal that you have been a good person, but nonetheless have avoided some important issues. This analysis enables you to experience the epiphany before the problem becomes a reality. It throws you into the future, shows you the results or consequences, and then brings you back (very quickly and safely) to the present where you can begin making changes.

If you feel your life lacks direction, stand up (or buckle down) and do something about it. Use a little introspection and unlock some of your enormous potential. Have no regrets, experience no loss of valuable time, just make and invest the time where you know you'll feel most rewarded. Use the values identification as a way to focus on your life's top priorities. I invite you to make a difference for yourself; in fact, I more than invite you, I challenge you—I dare you! I dare you to make the effort and experience the changes. It is easy to "chalk this one up as a good idea," but to take action means more effort; and more effort means more results.

Act this week on a top priority—even if it begins with a single phone call. List on paper the top priorities that come to mind.

Action Items

- Put a few actionable values to paper and consider what goals you can set to develop that priority.
- Make time to consider what thing(s) you want to do or how you want to make your mark before you leave planet Earth.
- Make something you fear overlooking in life a scheduled activity within the next few months.

GOALS

I know of no more encouraging fact than the
unquestionable ability of man to elevate his life
by conscious endeavor.

HENRY DAVID THOREAU

Your life is full of opportunities, and each day you are presented with an abundance of time to pursue them—so
much time, in fact, that you can't stay busy through an entire
day—you sleep through one third of it.

Unfortunately, where we have lots of freedom and discretionary time, we sometimes let days pass with the intention to do
something important, yet we find it difficult to make time for
that which is needed to accomplish our goals. However, it is
important to make time to address your future now because if
you don't, you risk drifting along your time line, missing out on
what life has to offer.

Webster's defines a goal as "an object or effort; an end or aim."
Create objectives for yourself to actively add value to your life.
Goals are important because they

- Place urgency on your priorities.
- Motivate you to act today.
- Create a time you can look forward to your achievements.

When you set goals you become more focused on what you
want; you find yourself less concerned with television, sleep, and

the social calendar because you are excited about the thought of achieving the goals. Although television and a social life do serve their purpose, they should be a *reward* and not an *escape*. If you seek a sense of accomplishment and personal growth, you will find yourself happier when gratified by your achievements, rather than frustrated as you spin time away on trivial things preoccupied by what you *should* be doing. Your life will have more meaning, and you will have more to show for your efforts as you meet the challenges of accomplishing goals within a specific time frame.

Tapping your potential is made possible by pushing yourself to use talents and achieve dreams that have a deadline.

All You Need Is a Pencil

Goal setting is a writing exercise. That's worth repeating: It is a *writing* exercise. Winners in life will tell you that goals are only effectively pursued when they are in writing because writing them down makes them tangible. It is a simple process of taking an abstract idea and reducing it to a concrete form. It is having the goal on paper that allows you to visualize the finished product and better plan the intermediate steps needed for its completion. Making adjustments to your strategy is simplified because, once again, moving the pieces around on paper is much easier than trying to do it in your head. Having the goal on paper also allows you to refer to something periodically to track and measure progress.

Written goals eliminate the stress of having to keep details in your head. Goal setting is not a science involving memory techniques. People who achieve goals rely on good *mechanics* and a systematic, disciplined approach to help them through the process. It is a roll-your-sleeves-up do-it-yourself project that requires creativity and logic—and a pencil and paper.

In seminars, I have asked people to raise their hands if they use a to-do list. Almost every hand in the room will be raised. They say, "I can't live without it!" They admit they need a to-do list by their side because

- They might forget what they have to do.
- They can refer to it throughout the day without having to memorize everything.
- Stress is decreased if they're not worried about forgetting.
- They love earning checkmarks.
- Additions and deletions are easily handled.

These are the very reasons why you want to put your goals on paper! Most people confuse goals with dreams, desires, wishes, and future aspirations—all of which will remain just out of reach until you clarify what you want and put it to paper. How can you expect to manage a two-year endeavor in your head if you can't get through the day without a to-do list? If you think you have goals—as described here—you should be able to *show* them to somebody.

I have conducted many goal-setting workshops with people from different backgrounds. Everyone is in hot pursuit of something. The following four steps will help you crystallize what you want and help you accomplish it:

1. Identifying your goals
2. Be specific
3. Use the right tools
4. Implement—take action

The first three criteria are best met, once again, by putting thoughts to paper. There will be some thinking and prioritization required. Criteria four will be left to the power of discipline and motivation. And a great motivator will be the ability to visualize your journey and the completion of your goal.

Tapping your potential involves successfully meeting all four of the above criteria.

Meeting the demands of these four criteria is made easy with the following four steps:

Step One: Identify Your Goals

It's easy to say, "I want it all," or "I want my life to change!" Most people can't decide which aspect of their lives to address. It helps to put a few ideas to paper and then pick one. Much of your decision of where to begin will be influenced by what values you identify as important. In the previous chapter, the concept of "actionable" values was discussed as the building blocks for your goals. Remember to prioritize so you address the more important values first. For example, financial status may need to be addressed before vacation options become possible. Or some of them may be mutually exclusive: You can't travel the world and climb the corporate ladder in the same year. This is a case of making choices and putting first things first.

I suggest focusing only on realistic possibilities. Goals should be interesting, creative, exciting, but not what you would perceive to be outlandish, randomly chosen, or conflicting with what you value. If the goal seems impractical or unattainable, put it on the back burner and begin with something more practical.

Many think that a goal needs to be a wild safari or some impressive endeavor. If it really isn't a burning desire, no matter how unique or creative it may be, it will soon be abandoned because the challenges you face simply won't be worth it. Pick what you want, and don't worry about all of the other possibilities for now. The following are some goals I'll never achieve:

- Go to medical school.
- Walk a tightrope in a circus.
- Paint the ceiling of a church.
- Sing with Pavarotti.
- Discover an unchartered island.
- Acquire the largest coin collection in America.

- Rebuild a '65 Mustang engine.
- Swim the English Channel.
- Star in a silent film.

That's okay. I have neither the desire nor the interest and, in some cases, the talent. The question becomes, once you eliminate the things that *won't* happen from your list of possibilities—realistic possibilities—are you investing your time and energy into the goals that you *do* want and that *are* within reach?

Step Two: Be Specific

People say, "I want to save some money to take a vacation some-where that's fun." Or "You'd like to buy a house and live some-where other than where you live now."

And when I ask, "But where do you want to go? Where do you want to live?" the answer is usually something like, "Any-where would be great!" The problem is if you don't know specif-ically what you want, you can't decide on the specifics of how you will get there. And if you can't visualize a specific finished product, it will not be very motivating.

You must know *where* you want to travel, *what* you want to do *when* you get there, *what* time of year you plan to go, etc. It helps to know the kind of house you plan to buy, in what particular part of the city you plan to live, and a price range in which to purchase, because you cannot effectively act on something unde-fined. You need specificity in what you want, and then the right tools to accomplish it.

Step Three: Use the Right Tools

When I ask how people address their goals, or through what kind of system, I often find another missing link: To manage a fairly detailed and complex process, people rely on a simple—or even nonexistent—system. Many people rely on memory, notes stuck to the refrigerator, a legal pad or nothing at all. We established that the to-do list is important in getting through the day, yet people think that a two-year endeavor can be managed in their head. A big mistake.

You must have a creative list of ideas on paper so you can systematically address them. The creative list of intermediate steps can be refined and sequenced as you identify and assign them dates. You find yourself in need of paper and pencil, a Franklin Day Planner, and sometimes a calculator. It truly becomes a hands-on project. You are now a long way away from having a simple aspiration in our head—you have developed a treasure map and are ready to take action.

Step Four: Implement—Take Action

If your first three criteria are in place, (identified goals, specificity, and good tools) there must be a desire and a motivation to make it happen. It is easy to sit on the couch and talk about all of the wonderful things you will have in life. It is an entirely different issue to *take action*. Sometimes it is a chronic case of procrastination, a lack of faith in our ability to succeed, or feeling as if your time to pursue a goal is crowded out by other activities. No matter how you try to get around it, you can't achieve goals unless all four criteria in the process are met.

Calendaring tasks into your planning system will provide an excellent reminder of what you should be doing; it provide focus, and allows you to track progress.

Taking action is a discipline that is developed over time. Doing small tasks, whether or not you feel like it, will help you grow stronger mentally and develop an ability to tackle bigger tasks when you need to.

The concept of tapping your potential assumes that you have a capacity or talent within you that can be released. This is accomplished by challenging yourself to accomplish goals.

Making the MOST of Your Dreams

Now it's time to go to work. What is needed is a logical thought process that will guide you through identifying what you want to the actual moment of implementation. If you can follow this process, much like moving through a flow chart, you will have written before you the entire strategy for creating something specific in your life. This MOST process is explained on the following pages as: Motivation, Objectives, Strategy, and Time frame.

Motivation: Why?

As mentioned in the chapter on purpose, knowing *why* you want to pursue your goals creates a sense of direction and focus. Working with purpose will increase both your confidence and your motivation.

You attack the goal with greater diligence if you are reminded of the fact that this is a top priority in your life—tied to one of your values.

> I keep six honest
>   serving men
> (They taught me all
>   I knew);
> Their names are What
>   and Why and When
> And How and Where
>   and Who.
>   RUDYARD KIPLING

Lets look at some of those "actionable" values from the previous chapter and use those as a basis for goal setting. For example:

We read. *Why?* Because we value intellectual growth.

We budget our money. *Why?* Because we value financial stability.

We give our time or money to volunteer organizations. *Why?* Because we value charity.

We travel. *Why?* Because we value relaxing and experiencing new cultures.

You should evaluate what values are currently most important to you. This list will motivate you to set specific objectives.

For example, a comfortable retirement is something that everyone wants. However, college students have other, more pressing, issues to address: paying off loans, getting a job, saving for a car, etc. As they grow older, retirement will move up the list of priorities. As a teenager, there may be no need to ask, "If retiring comfortably today is important, what should I do about it this week?"

On the other hand, if buying a car and finding a good job are motivators, there will be a need to set some specific objectives. The process of goal setting involves clarifying your motivators, and identifying specific goals that would logically follow.

Objectives: What?

What is best defined as determining a future objective, a complete picture of what you want on a specific date in the future. It will require some intermediate steps for accomplishment, as opposed to a task that is normally a single event.

If a goal is well thought out, it will need to meet the following criteria:

- Specificity—no vague ideas of what you want
- Time-framed—not someday, when you have time, or soon
- Written—on paper as opposed to committed to memory
- Measurable—quantifiable or tangible

The benefit of having the goal on paper is that it is now concrete and represents something important. You now have items to refer to as a blueprint for accomplishing that objective.

For example:

- Saving $10,000 in two years demonstrates your value for financial security.
- Buying a home in two years demonstrates your value for a certain standard of living.
- Traveling to Rome demonstrates your value for learning about Renaissance art.

- Organizing a food drive demonstrates your feelings about charity.

All of these objectives are pursued because of what you value. You best determine goals for these values by asking, "If these are the values, *what* can I do about them?" You best achieve the goals by asking, "If these are my goals, *how* will I accomplish them?"

Strategy: How?

How is best defined as identifying the approach and details needed to complete the goal. It involves identifying the many tasks that contribute to the accomplishment of what you want. These intermediate steps will be periodically scheduled into daily routines and implemented over time.

Referring back to the goals examples, saving $10,000 in two years will involve:

- Budgeting
- Savings plan
- Periodic electronic transfer at your bank
- Opening a special bank account

Buying a home in two years will involve:

- An appointment with a real estate agent
- Researching newspapers
- Starting a savings plan
- Selling the current residence

Traveling to Greece in two years will involve:

- Scheduling time off
- Calling a travel agent

- Applying for a passport
- Learning something about the country

All of these steps will be scheduled over time and become part of your daily task list. You best implement and act on your intermediate steps and activate the goal by asking, "If these are my intermediate steps, *when* am I going to do something about them?" Here are the steps, now let's do it! Asking *when* is critical because the question *when* brings about commitment and forces you to refer to a planning system. *When* conquers vague language like *soon* and *someday*.

Time Frame: When?

When is best defined as choosing the best *dates* in your day planners for implementation. They will be incorporated into each day's list of activities and ideally become the center, or core, of your priorities around which everything else is scheduled.

One Step at a Time

Sometimes we are a bit discouraged at the scope of the goal and the expected time for its accomplishment. It seems that our endeavor is just too big or that it may take forever to accomplish. As a result, we set the goal aside, thereby ensuring that it never happens.

A simple idea that will change your mind-set is to forget about accomplishing the goal. Don't try to tackle the entire goal; work only on the intermediate steps—and only one step at a time.

Dick Bass, a successful businessman and entrepreneur in energy and building resorts, accomplished an incredible feat. He and some friends climbed the highest mountains on each of the seven continents. Here's a man who, with little mountain climbing experience, decided to do what no man had ever done before: Climb Aconcagua in South America, Everest in Asia, McKinley in North America, Kilimanjaro in Africa, Elbrus in Europe, Vinson in Antarctica, and Kosciusko in Australia. At the time, Dick Bass was fifty-one years old.

I heard Dick Bass speak at his Utah ski resort, Snowbird. He detailed what was running through his mind and the challenges everyone on the expedition faced as they worked on their conquests. It was both an incredible and funny story as he narrated the adventure with amazing pictures shown on a slide projector, an adventure he details in his book *Seven Summits,* along with co-author and mountaineering companion Frank Wells, then president of Warner Brothers.

I had a chance to speak with Dick after his presentation, and he mentioned that there are as many metaphors present in climbing a mountain as there are in living life—addressing big challenges, dealing with the unexpected, overcoming fear, persistence, desire, faith, teamwork, motivation, and a whole host of psychological exercises, including visualization—that made his phenomenal achievement possible.

I asked him if he ever felt overwhelmed or intimidated as he hiked over rocks and through ravines.

He said no.

I asked if he focused on short-term goals like getting to the next camp.

He said no.

"How did you do it?"

He replied, "One step at a time, one foot in front of the other, and I never quit."

I have no immediate plans to climb a mountain, much less the highest of them on each of the seven continents. In fact, I was tired after just watching the slide presentation. But I realized his philosophy has direct application to my life: Identify what you want, and then do something about it *consistently.*

Referring to our goal-setting approach thus far, notice how the expedition follows the MOST formula.

Why were Bass and Wells motivated? Because they enjoyed challenges. Both had been very successful in business, and they thought they would try applying their business philosophy of anything being possible to the challenge of climbing a mountain.

Dick Bass had built a ski resort that took fourteen years to finish. Frank Wells ran a movie studio. Both knew the long struggle that could exist in a business endeavor. This would be a different challenge. Bass said, "It's me and the mountain, and that's it. There are no bankers or regulatory officials telling me what I can and can't do. It's just me and my own two feet, my own physical strength, and my own mental resolve."

He pursued his value for challenge and adventure. That was the *motivation* for the expedition.

What was the *objective*? Climb not just a mountain, or the biggest, but *all* of the biggest on *all* seven continents. No one had ever done it—professional or amateurs. And at their age (Frank was a few months away from fifty), with little experience, they were sure to face many challenges and adventures. That's a respectable goal.

What was their *strategy*? There were many little details that had to come together to make this expedition possible. It involved research, training, planning, talking with locals and anyone else who would contribute to the success of the project—no doubt a carefully planned strategy since many lives were at stake. The only task left would be developing time lines and dates for implementation. In other words, *when* should they get started?

A Puzzling Analogy

Accomplishing important tasks is made possible by protecting them from some of the more trivial tasks that can steal our time. The task that contributes to the goal must get top priority or it will continually get crowded out and quite possibly never happen. It's a lot like a puzzle I bought in Italy.

A few years ago, I bought a wooden, hand-carved puzzle in

Milan, Italy. A simple souvenir that, when assembled, is shaped like a perfect rectangular block. It looked easy enough.

Like any puzzle, it practically falls apart in your hand when you disassemble it and takes about six months and substantial hair loss to put it back together. But I figured out the secret. There is a center piece that serves as a core to the rectangle— around which all of the other pieces must be fitted. If you try to stack them, or piece them in a normal sequence, you cannot push the center piece in between them. It is as if the side pieces hang onto the sides of the main core of the rectangle. Once you learn this, the puzzle is simple. Simply put the core piece on the table, and one piece at a time, hang the side pieces on almost as attachments. And so it is with intermediate steps.

The key to putting together the pieces of your goal will be making the tasks that contribute to the goal the central piece or the core of the day or evening. If other "pieces" come first, there won't be any room for the most important piece: the one that acts as the core—the task that is in line with your goals. Many times trivial activities, social phone calls, and indecision absorb much of the day, and you find yourself torn between sleeping at ten o'clock in the evening or buckling down for the project— usually sleep is justified at the end of the day and will win. Unfortunately, the trivial crowds out the vital. If this process becomes chronic, you never get results.

Tapping your potential means you must give higher priority to those activities that will help you reach your goals—in place of other activities that appeal to you at the moment.

From Why to When In Boston

Let me walk you through the process from start to finish with a recent experience in my life.

One of my values is cultural awareness and fun. I enjoy traveling to different parts of the United States and the world, experiencing other cultures and people. I like the adventure of vacationing and the enjoyable break from my normal busy routine. Because of these values, I decided to address them by doing something specific. In other words, if "culture and fun" are important to me, *what* specifically could I do to act on it?

I brainstormed with a college friend of mine about taking a vacation. We decided that Boston would be both a cultural experience and fun. This would require more focus in

> Never mistake motion for action.
>
> ERNEST HEMINGWAY

terms of dates and the length of the vacation, etc. The goal became "In July, 1992, we will travel to two locations in Massachusetts: Boston, and Cape Cod, for seven days, and I will have $2,000 set aside to make this possible."

Once we agreed on the big picture, the next question was, "How do we pull all of this together?" We had to think about *how* we would address the details and which one of us would do the legwork. Our *how*, in no particular order, looked something like this:

- Research airfares.
- Block out seven days in July.
- Start setting aside funds.
- Buy brochures so we know something about the city and what to do once we arrive there.
- Purchase luggage.
- Clear work calendar for that week.
- Purchase tickets to a sporting event while visiting.

We outlined the number of steps needed to make it happen, delegated some items to others joining us on the trip, and we talked periodically to share information about the vacation.

The actual implementation took place when we decided to purchase the tickets. We had to coordinate exactly *when* we would contact one another for credit-card numbers, and who would call the hotel and reserve rooms.

All the pieces did pull together nicely, and the vacation was a success. However, if the *why*, *what*, and *how* were considered, but nobody took action by asking *when*, we would only have a picture in our minds of what Boston would be like instead of photographs now placed in the album.

Tapping your potential is made easy when following the MOST formula.

The Importance of Solitude Therapy

A big obstacle people face when thinking about their future is that their vision can be limited and obscured by details of just getting through the day. We never seem to get a break. Each day presents a workload that makes the thought of getting ahead seem like a science fiction fantasy.

Take the case of a person I met while speaking at a large conference in Phoenix. I'll call him Jim.

Jim approached me at the break after my presentation and was clearly motivated to do a few things about his career outside of the normal scope of responsibilities. He then commented that if only he had some time to clear his thoughts, organize a few things, finish one of his already-started projects, and basically play catch-up, he'd be okay. He said, "Sometimes the list seems so long and so overwhelming that it makes you want to set everything aside and just not think about it." He had some creative ideas but never felt like he had any time to act on them.

He said, "I seem to go from work, to the children, to cooking dinner, to preparing for the next day, to the news, to the bed. And for everything I fail to do during the week, it becomes a weekend task that encroaches upon my relaxation time. Before I know it, Sunday evening sets in, and away I go for another five-day stretch!"

After speaking more with Jim, I admitted that with a travel schedule, work responsibilities, and what's left of my social life, I, too, can find myself overtaxed in the daily schedule and forced to make some choices.

I asked, "What do your weekend activities normally include?"

"Usually relaxing, watching a ball game, running a few errands, a little yard work, taking it easy with the family."

"Do you ever have any time to yourself?"

"Sure, I get up a couple of hours earlier than everyone in the house, and then my wife will take the kids with her if she goes shopping."

We soon discovered that there are pockets of time he has for himself to chip away at the large list of responsibilities that appear to be adding up. The key is to know exactly where to go and what to do with the moments of discretionary time he has. It all boils down to the discipline of having specific objectives and being able to take some action. Jim will never get closer to doing things for himself if he decides to "just not think about it," nor will those tasks just get up and walk out of his life. Periodically we must spend a little quiet time—even at the expense of something we enjoy doing—addressing important issues. We need some solitude therapy.

> Solitude is as needful to the imagination as society is wholesome for the character.
>
> JAMES RUSSELL LOWELL

Also, we must make a priority—the core of the puzzle—time to do something about the very tasks that are barriers to moving on to our goals.

You must clear away the number of little things to create time for the important things.

I have found that mini-vacations can be rejuvenating and productive. I'm not talking about a short hop to Hawaii to sort a few things out, but about quiet "pockets" of solitude for thinking, or using a business trip as a brief sabbatical to put a few things in order. When you are away from distractions, your concentration level is deeper, your imagination is allowed "off of its leash," you develop ideas more completely, and you subconsciously put things in perspective.

Over the years, I have learned to make use of the time I spend traveling on airplanes for productive, therapeutic thinking. While many people look out the window, watch the in-flight movie, or try to sleep, I have developed the habit of "thinking and sorting."

There is nothing wrong with relaxing on an airplane. However, if the daily chaos of home and work life is distracting, use the hours of travel time (van pool, car pool, train, bus, car commute) to review goals; track progress; read that book; list home-improvement activities that must be addressed; schedule personal items, such as dentist and car maintenance, tax preparation ideas, new business and income ideas; write a letter to a friend; send one thank-you note; or complete your expense report. The list of possibilities goes on.

I have the same pockets of time that Jim has, as well as those few hours a week of "flight therapy" that help me put many things in perspective and decrease stress. Much of this book was written en route to teaching seminars all around the country. The value of solitude therapy will be expressed through much of the clear thinking we do and the little tasks we accomplish, which do add up. Clearing them out of the way will make room for us to pursue our dreams. Then we need to maintain and balance that scenario—keeping goals the core of the puzzle.

It seems that in today's world with more people, mass transportation, bus rides, subways, cars, people, phones, faxes, beepers, voice mail, e-mail, and portable computers, we are denied the freedom and time to stop and consider how well our time is being spent. William Wordsworth, one of the great Romantic poets of the early nineteenth century, wrote about it almost two hundred years ago in his poem "The World Is Too Much With Us." He feels that much of nature has been "up-gathered" and removed from our lives, and with it the very therapy and spiritual balance we receive from nature's company:

We have given our hearts away, a sordid boon!
This sea that bares her bosom to the moon;
The winds that will be howling at all hours,
Are up-gathered now like sleeping flowers;
For this, for everything, we are out of tune . . .

Whether you simply need a break, or need a change, or need to tap your potential, the value of removing yourself from chaos and returning to solitude (and even nature) has been endorsed by poets, psychologists, the Bible, and travel agencies (the last one has another motive). Use your day planner to schedule time away from work and even family periodically, and you'll return with a fresh outlook, perspective, and greater motivation.

In order to tap your potential, you must focus on your goals. And focus is made possible by eliminating distractions in an environment conducive to clear thinking.

Action Items

- Process a value through the MOST formula and see what action you can take this week.
- Gather the tools you need to enhance the mechanics in goal setting (*Franklin Day Planner*, calculator, research material, pens, pencils, and a telephone).
- Schedule some solitude therapy (two hours or two days) and clear the slate of little things that will make room for the pursuit of more important things.

MAPPING YOUR STRATEGY

"Cheshire-puss, would you tell me, please, which way I
ought to go from here?"
"That depends a good deal on where you want to get to,"
said the cat.
"I don't care much where—" said Alice.
"Then it doesn't matter which way you go." said the cat.

LEWIS CARROLL

A critical part of tapping your potential is to turn the *desire* of getting what you want into a *plan of action* for what you want. Once you are focused on a destination, you must plan how to get there. You must develop a specific blueprint that will detail and put in motion your desire to achieve a level of success.

The plan is as basic a component in the success formula as arithmetic is to any form of math: Without an understanding of how it works, it makes moving on to more sophisticated exercises difficult. If adding and subtracting seem trivial to you, but geometry, algebra, trigonometry, and calculus are very important, you'll become frustrated very soon. People make the same mistake with their lives: Goals, dreams, and desires are a great source of motivation but are never fully realized if the means for achievement—the plan—gets overlooked. Plans are critical because they

- Make you more results-oriented.
- Detail what you need to do each day.

- Decrease the number of urgencies you will face.
- Ensure that a little time each day is invested in your goals.

Webster's dictionary defines a plan as "a diagram showing the arrangement of a structure." The plan for tapping your potential consists of arranging a sequence of events you feel will bring you desired results over time. *The plans must be in writing!* If they are in your head, then part of the challenge in getting through the day will be working the list from memory. Planning is a writing exercise (much like goal setting) that takes the abstract and makes it concrete—it transforms it into something you can refer throughout the day.

Blueprinting the Strategy

If you think of developing the plan as a simple list used to get through the day, it's not a lot of fun. If you think of it as trivial, you'll put trivial things on the list. When you think of it as a *strategy* for living each day to its fullest, the plan takes on more significance—it's not something you use just to get through the day. It should include a few items, every day, that contribute to attaining desired results in your future. It is a tool that is essential in your quest for tapping potential.

Plan Like a General

Picture yourself a Norman Schwarzkopf with a major mission. What would you need to succeed? Achieving goals is as important to you as any mission on this earth. How would you get dressed for the event if it really mattered to you? Fatigues, sweats, jeans, a suit? How would you draft and design your course of action? Would you work in a "war room" complete with maps, miniature models, a compass, weather patterns, time zones, language translations, radio equipment, fax, car phone, hand-held phone, laptop computer, radar, beeper, short-wave radio, night vision equipment, and dried foods? Do you see the connection between gearing up for a war, and getting ready for a day at the office or even attacking your future? What would you need for empowerment to ensure a victory? What strategies would you plan to implement? How much of life's potential might you be overlooking if you do not have a well-thought-out plan complete with the tools to make it happen?

If you don't have a strategy to tap your potential, you will overlook huge reservoirs that could lie dormant forever.

Your ROI (Return on Investment)

Many people feel like they don't have time to plan—"I'm so busy, who has the time?" Some people perceive planning as preventing them from acting. But the reality of planning is that it is not merely time well *spent*, it is time well *invested*. A few moments up front to clarify the day or the week will be returned back to you in the form of increased confidence, reduced stress, deeper sleep, and time saved backtracking. You will work much faster when you are able to sys-

> Let our advanced worrying become advanced thinking and planning.
> SIR WINSTON CHURCHILL

tematically work through a plan rather than having to constantly re-evaluate and recall things you've stored in your short-term memory. So, get away from distractions and put your daily objectives on paper!

I gave a speech for a large bank in Southern California a few years ago, and afterwards the client offered me a ride to the airport. Due to some uncontrollable events, the speech ended twenty minutes later than planned. I was already cutting it a little close in making my flight but figured as long as I didn't have to drive, I'd get dropped off curbside at my terminal, allowing me to make the flight with a few minutes to spare.

Dave, my driver to the airport, was in good spirits as we left the hotel and made our way to the car. We soon discovered that the parking garage was already full of cars in line trying to leave the facility. Apparently, one of the other conventions at the hotel finished a few minutes earlier than we had and was now creating a minor gridlock in the parking structure. We soon joined the queue.

We made casual small talk as we inched our way toward the parking kiosk. Casual and relaxed on the outside, inside I was a complete wreck as I pictured myself stuck inside the parking structure, joining a few million other cars on the Santa Monica freeway, and then running alongside United Flight 1128 as passengers on the plane pointed and laughed.

When we finally left the structure I felt I could breathe again. Dave continued to tell me about his daughter's incredible ability to finger paint eucalyptus trees, and I nodded as if mesmerized by how that could actually be possible. I had also contemplated screaming just to see how he would handle the change of pace.

After we made a few lefts and rights, I had the feeling he wasn't sure how to access the freeway. Between his sentences I could hear periodic mumbling that sounded something like, "I could have sworn . . . oh, c'mon . . . that's the problem with road construction . . . why wouldn't they have a sign that said 'West' . . . hold on . . . this must be it." I looked up and wondered if I could fit though the sun roof and make a run for it.

I asked if he had a map somewhere in the car so I could navigate while he attempted to drive. His response left me speechless. He said, "Well, the problem is it's in the trunk." To which I replied, "So, does the trunk open?" To which he replied, "Do you think we have time to stop?" I had to hold back the tears.

In the end, we did grab a map, we did make it to the airport on time—although I think I looked a little older than I did that morning. The point here relative to planning is that he didn't know where he was going, and when I suggested looking at a map, instead of him seeing that as a *solution* to our problems, he saw it as a possible *obstacle* in getting us to the airport on time.

Taking time to plan ahead always makes things run more smoothly, and ultimately saves wasted time.

A Creative Process: Visualization

Another way of thinking about this otherwise "dry" science of planning is to use Alan Lakein's approach. In his book *How to Get Control of Your Time and Your Life*, Lakein describes planning as "bringing the future into the present, so you can do something about it now." This process of visualization is priceless because it allows you to familiarize yourself with the day's events before they get to you. It allows you to experience the future in your imagination and prepare for activities that could be overlooked or become crises later.

> Every moment you spend in planning, you save three to four moments in the execution of the plans.
>
> CRAWFORD GREENWALT

If you have ever

- Dressed yourself in your mind before a vacation
- Role-played before a sales call
- Second-guessed questions to an exam or job interview so your answers would flow smoothly

you have taken part in a visualization exercise. You have experienced the "actual" event in your mind first (and possibly several times) before doing it in reality. You've now had time to make mistakes, correct mistakes, recognize possible setbacks, and prevent them by thinking steps through beforehand. One of Dr. Stephen Covey's "habits" from *The Seven Habits of Highly Effective People* is "begin with the end in mind first." Have a picture of what the desired outcome looks like first, and then begin the journey. It is our preview of coming attractions that simplifies the visualization exercise and brings to mind the myriad details in the strategy.

Shopping Hungry

Have you ever made a trip to the grocery store with a general
idea of what you needed? Ever tried doing it when you're hungry? Suppose you need soap, eggs,
chicken, and a few dairy products. But
because you're hungry and didn't start
with a list of the things you needed,
you purchase ten pounds of potato
chips, dip, hot dogs, exotic almond
spread, minced artichoke hearts, and a

> Planning is the process of
> outguessing and outsmarting
> failure.
>
> ROBERT D. GILBREATH

box of 10,000 mint-flavored toothpicks. What happened? You
got side-tracked and returned home with a lot of supplies—but
not the right ones. Sure, you can say you did your shopping, but
you weren't very effective judging by the outcome.

I have watched many people make this same mistake around
the office. Because they feel burdened by their main responsibilities, they rush into the office, drop everything, grab a cup of coffee, and all they know is that they'd better get started—on what,
exactly, they almost don't care, as long as they stay occupied and
do something!

So rather than develop and then systematically chip away at a
plan, they do what is in front of them, whatever they get asked to
do, or whatever looks good at that particular moment—a classic
example of reactive behavior. They spend three minutes on voice
mail, two minutes shuffling through the "in" basket, tear open a
few letters, bring something up on the computer screen, attempt
to organize their desk, and then start the routine all over again in
the same cycle.

If we asked this person if they took time to plan their day
(much like asking our friend Dave if he wouldn't mind referring
to the map), we would probably elicit the response, "Oh, no, I
barely have time to breathe, much less set aside time to plan my
day." Once again, the big oversight is failing to see how planning
will solve the problems, not add one more to the list that will

detract from productivity. Planning creates feelings of confidence and focus. You change from trying to do *everything right* to doing the *right things*.

Life Is a Grocery Store

If you don't have an occasional "grocery list" for life or the ability to identify on paper what you want, you'll leave with something else. We are just as "hungry" for a sense of accomplishment in our day as we sometimes are in the grocery store for food. This

> Planning is bringing the future into the present so that you can do somethingh about it now.
> ALAN LAKEIN

desire to get something done may drive us to get trivial things accomplished, rather than the truly important things that contribute to our goals. We have many selections from which to choose off the "shelves of life." What do you want? Of course, you can't have everything, and some of the things you do experience weren't planned for, but it shouldn't entirely be a guessing game. With limited time and resources, you need to make your visits to the store effective ones. Each day, you enter through the doors of life with an idea of what you want, where it is, and how you plan to pay for it. Get what you want faster by developing an effective plan.

What Is Sprezzatura?

We need to consider the misleading presence and poise some people carry with them. What is that casual, peaceful, carefree quality that many of the wealthy and successful people have about them? Who are the people who appear to be so pampered, relaxed, and seem to be enjoying so much in life? Who are the upscale Joneses who take vacations regularly and have the nice house with all the amenities and 3.2 children? Who are the people at school and at work who get the job done without appearing to be stressed or "tapped out?" These are the individuals who work hard, long, and smart.

Sprezzatura is a literary term defined as "the seeming ease and negligence with which one meets the demands of complex and exacting rules of behavior." In simple terms, it is the talent and gift of doing something very difficult but making it look simple. Many pianists appear to be gliding their fingers across the keys while beautiful music fills the room; professional golfers like Jack Nicklaus and Gary Player make it look so easy; Fred Astaire and Ginger Rogers danced as one. These are examples of sprezzatura that make observing the performance so enjoyable.

In our day-to-day activities it is easy to admire those that have big titles, nice cars, a wonderful family, and a little extra cash. Keep in mind that this "seeming ease and negligence" are really the tangible manifestations of what financial, career, and daily planning can bring. These people probably work hard and smart every day—starting early, working into the evenings, and giving a lot of thought to issues that many people never consider or care to consider. This is not to suggest that those who don't have a lot of material goods don't work or think hard; and there is also the possibility that the person who appears to be doing well won the lottery or received a sizeable inheritance. But it seems

> Every man is the architect of his own fortune.
>
> SALLUST

that the quality of life is tied in many ways to financial freedom and the ability to pursue things worth pursuing because of the number of available resources. We can't all be Rockefellers or necessarily care to be. But we can experience more happiness and riches in our lives through acquiring the habit of discipline.

The important point is that people who do the things they want and have a happy life are people who, in most cases, think a lot about making it happen. They have proactively tapped their potential in certain areas and it shows. Planning and mapping out the day is an integral part of pursuing a goal, getting daily results, and preparing for the future. I once read that "the only place success comes before work is in the dictionary." Consistent planning and hard work will bring you consistent results over time. Each day will serve as a building block for the next, and you'll experience an enjoyable journey toward your dreams.

A plan is a strategy designed to address activities that will help you tap your potential.

Action Items

- Set aside time every day for planning.
- Plan tomorrow's day tonight and visualize each of the events you'll encounter.
- Change the nature of your plan from a maintenance list to a list that includes items connected to your values and goals.

BREAKING TRADITION

Tradition is what you resort to when you don't
have the time or the money to do it right.

KENT HERBERT ADLER

Over the years we have developed different routines, habits, and patterns of behavior that have become our standard method of going about our lives. After these routines "settle in" and have proven themselves to be at least adequately effective, we hesitate to change our ways and try something new. Why should we? Why take our time-tested means of behaving and replace them with untried new ones?

Although it is human to cling to something we know works, it may be divine to pursue something new, despite the perception that it is risky and unchartered territory. What if there is a better mousetrap? Is it possible to do it better, faster, more effectively, or with less stress and have more fun?

One of our challenges is to recondition ourselves (refer to your belief card-file system under *C* for Change) to change the belief that "if it ain't broke, don't fix it," to "although this 'ain't broke' there may be a better alternative." The typewriter "ain't broke," but the computer is still a better alternative.

Tapping your potential requires you to try new things and change some behaviors.

The other challenge is to overcome fear. This fear is manifested by a strong concern for trying something new or foreign and having to venture toward strange frontiers. As a result, we deny ourselves new, productive, and perhaps

If you deliberately do the thing that you fear, the death of fear is certain.

RALPH WALDO EMERSON

more enjoyable experiences, and we subject ourselves to stagnation at the expense of personal growth. Our world becomes smaller because we limit the number of experiences available to us by doing the same things over and over. Our options are fewer in number because we have not been open to so many other choices.

Jim Newman originated the idea of the psychological "comfort zone." In his book *Release Your Brakes!* he defines a comfort zone as "the kind of environment in which you feel at ease, relatively free of tension—one's image of 'the way things are supposed to be.'" In other words, comfort zones are purely psychological—they reside only in the mind of the individual. They are "one's image" or one's perception of the way things ought to look, feel, or exist according to our own set of rules. Much of our untapped potential will remain just out of reach if we can't get a little creative and part with the familiar to find new ways to unleash it.

For example, if a civic organization you belong to wants to reach a large part of the community with an important message on crime prevention, how could you do it? You might do a mailing as it is usually handled. But what if you decided to call a meeting as a way to personalize it and have greater impact? What if running a community meeting was a way for you to increase the impact of the message, but it was never tried before? How would you feel about speaking in front of a group of about three hundred citizens? Beside the fact that it is out of the ordinary, would that be enough reason to drop the idea entirely? Would you miss out on a major opportunity simply because you are required to do something you don't usually do—something outside your comfort zone?

There are many examples of being put in new situations where we may not have a track record, yet a lot is at stake—not in terms of what could be lost if we fail, rather what we fail to gain if we don't take the chance.

I'm Guilty

In the summer of 1994, I traveled to Scandinavia with some friends. None of us had traveled to that part of Europe before, so it was sure to be a new and different experience for all involved. We did what we could to learn more about the countries, their customs, culture, and currency, but what you can learn and what you actually experience are very different.

Part of the stress (or excitement, depending on how you look at it) of travel is temporarily not having control of your life. You need other people for help, translations, maps, and even have a dependency on specific foreign exchange locations for money. We clearly were not as free to "do our thing" in Scandinavia as we would be somewhere in our own country. It was both leaving a comfort zone and entering an exciting, new part of the world.

Although we claimed we looked forward to experiencing the different foods and new city, after several days of walking and visiting and observing (classic stereotypical tourists—cameras included), we all looked forward to returning to where we felt comfortable even if it was the hotel. After hours of bratwurst (served with a slice of bread and ketchup on a piece of waxed paper), their version of a soft drink (I believe it was called a "Jolly! Cola"), I looked forward to something more familiar. When we passed a McDonalds, I pleaded with my friends to stop and indulge just like I did as a kid every time my father drove us past a Dairy Queen (remember the soft ice cream with the swirl?) Those golden arches looked better to me than any landmark I had seen to that point.

The burgers and fries tasted exactly as they do at home. I felt like a kid again as I enthusiastically ran from the counter to a table with my Big Mac, drink, fries, apple pie, and McNuggets, wearing my new Ronald McDonald hat and Hamburglar pin. My friends, to my surprise, sat at a different table.

We flipped through television channels at the hotel searching for an English-speaking station. It was a great relief to find a CNN news broadcast and even an old T.V. episode of *I Dream of Jeannie* was better than any local broadcast. We all have a tendency to gravitate toward the familiar.

You don't need to travel to faraway lands to feel the desire for remaining in a comfort zone. You consciously or subconsciously move toward one every day of your life. Although spending time in a comfort zone is understandable, you should not let the need for the familiar override the benefit of trying something new. In other words, in terms of tapping your potential, your desire for changing circumstances and reaching goals should be greater than the need to stick with the old routine.

You See Them Every Day

The following are examples of comfort zones you experience:

Social: You know it feels good to be with friends and family. If you are with people you know whose company you enjoy, you tend to be at ease, free of stress, you feel safe and trustful—all desirable emotions. However, it is not always possible to have these people with you as you pursue your dreams. Joining clubs, associations, committees, and going to school in the evenings may require you to be "the new guy" in class for a while. If you can cope with temporarily being outside a social comfort zone, you can bring yourself the benefits and opportunities of a new learning experience.

For example, "networking" is an important part of personal and professional growth. It may require you to feel that awkward initial introduction with people, but soon those feelings will disappear. As you meet new people and develop relationships, soon those "new" people become part of the comfort zone as they change from acquaintances to associates and friends.

People have a tremendous amount of information and wisdom to offer—wisdom that can be of help to you in tapping your potential. There is much

> We have been born to associate with our fellow man, and to join in community with the human race.
> CICERO

to gain from both a relationship and information standpoint. Make efforts to be more open, outgoing, and involved. A decision to not tap other people's resources and information is limiting and inhibitive. To confidently develop relationships with people and seek out their ideas is liberating and constructive in your efforts to tap potential.

Tapping potential requires a broad base of people in your social comfort zone.

Geographical: There are several levels of geographical comfort zones: your home, your neighborhood, your community, your county, your city, your

> Home is where the heart is.
> PLINY

state, your continent, and Earth. Anywhere you have lived for a while becomes familiar to you. You have local restaurants you enjoy, the dry cleaners, freeways, shortcuts, etc. A geographical comfort zone, at any level, becomes "your world." This is natural. But what if you had to travel or change residences to advance in your profession? Hopefully, a seemingly small issue like familiarity with a location would not be a deciding factor in whether or not you pursue your objective.

Try a new place for lunch; consider an alternate route to work; weigh the advantages of moving to a community that would better you as a person or a family. Changing will involve a break from nostalgia; but breaking away from nostalgia may be a small price to pay compared to the benefit of making the change.

Take the case of a friend of mine we'll call Elizabeth, who lived about seven miles away from my home. She recently bought a nice house closer to where I live and is now only about a mile away. We were together in my car one day and had a casual conversation about the dry cleaners we'd just passed—the one I happen to visit each week.

I complimented the service and professionalism I receive from my establishment. She mentioned she used another dry cleaners, closer to where she used to live. When I suggested she try the one closer to her new home, she was afraid to "risk" her good clothes at my dry cleaners. The conversation went something like this:

"Elizabeth, you should give this dry cleaners a chance; they've been great to me for almost five years now."

"Why would I go to this one?"

"Because you live about a half a mile away."

"But ABC cleaners is where I always go."

"Okay . . . but you don't live near them anymore."

"Yeah . . . but I'm used to them. I always go there."

I asked about her cleaner's service and we compared notes. His store is open from 8 A.M. to 6 P.M. Monday through Saturday; my cleaners is open 6 A.M. to 9 P.M. seven days a week. Her cleaners charges fifty cents more per shirt and a dollar more per suit; my cleaners has a stated "it's-perfect-or-it's-free" policy, hers doesn't; mine has same-day service available, hers doesn't; mine is a half a mile away from where she now lives, hers is almost seven miles away. I thought I'd convinced her to try my dry cleaners.

"Wow, that sounds like a great place," she commented. "But . . . I always go to the other one . . . you know . . . that's *my* dry cleaners."

I never worry about maintaining my friendship with Elizabeth. I have a feeling that if she moved from Southern California to Denver, we'd still see each other once a week—we could have lunch over by *her* dry cleaners.

The benefits of leaving a comfort zone often outweigh those of staying in a comfort zone.

Financial: How much do you earn? Now cut that number in half—how does it feel? Think of your current income again. Now double it—how does that feel? Better, I'm sure. But is it hard to believe that it is yours? For a while it would be, but after a few weeks you would become accustomed to it, and that new number would become your new standard; and all of the material things it could buy would eventually change your standard of living. Believe it or not, what you feel you should be earning sometimes creates the behavior to ensure that you do earn that amount—no more, no less.

There is the old story about people in sales who spend the first couple of weeks of the month coasting along playing golf, leaving the office early, etc. They are then left with the task of generating the numbers in the final days of the month. And because they apply themselves, they somehow squeak by. They make the numbers in the quota range where they feel they "ought to be."

> All wealth is the product of labor.
>
> JOHN LOCKE

The converse of this story is also true. If a sales associate is very fortunate the first couple of weeks in the month and makes a few sales with big numbers, he may take the final days of the month to play tennis, leave work early, etc. In other words the behavior was modified (he stopped selling) to leave the numbers for the month where he felt they "ought to be." Anything less is unacceptable, but the behavior subconsciously shuts down in order to never do better.

Stretch and find ways to earn more or save more than you normally would.

You'll never change what you earn until you change your concept of what you "ought to be" earning.

Intellectual: People like to discuss things in which they appear to be knowledgeable. If you studied geography for four years in college, and geography comes up in a discussion at

> For knowledge, too, is itself a power.
>
> FRANCIS BACON

dinner, you feel at ease and comfortable with the subject matter. You may hesitate to speak if lost Chinese civilizations becomes the topic—you may even become uncomfortable with what we do not know. Rather than being inquisitive, you become intimidated to the point of leaving the table. And that's the point! Never deny yourself the opportunity to learn something new simply because it is different than something with which you are familiar. Be an intellectual sponge. Soak in everything that you can about the world around you. A room full of people know far more collectively that we can ever expect to learn individually, so stick around. Never be afraid to ask questions. People avoid asking for answers or clarification because of the fear of looking like dummies. They never venture away from subjects they can discuss intelligently because they think they will be perceived by others as unintelligent. Not true!

Part of the wisdom in tapping your potential is to understand that sometimes you don't know *what you don't know*. Sometimes other people help you find your potential, or provide a way for you to develop or cultivate a potential (a piano teacher, a football coach, or a manager). Reading books, attending seminars, or listening to tapes are ways to expand horizons and enlighten you as to not only how to tap innate potential, but to discover what some of those many potentials may be. To deny yourself these opportunities is to walk through the library of life with blinders on, going to the same set of books at each visit. Your mind is a tremendous storage area that thirsts for new information. Step into different arenas, intellectual or otherwise, that will feed the mind and open doors.

Tapping your potential is made possible by expanding your intellectual horizons.

Who's Doing the Wagging?

We will always have comfort zones. The message is not to avoid them, but to be aware of the ones that are limiting or blocking the path to our potential. In other words, when the comfort zone defines your goals, it is tantamount to having the tail wag the dog.

> Sometimes it's not enough to do your best, you must do what is required.
> SIR WINSTON CHURCHILL

Remember that when you try something new, the newness soon fades away and will become part of your newly expanded comfort zone. For that reason, your comfort zones are continually broadening and evolving. That can be a redeeming quality for pushing yourself to try new things—it is only new for a short while; then it becomes familiar territory.

For example, if your work required you to live in Chicago for six months, and you've never been to Chicago, things may seem a bit strange to you for a while: different roads, street signs, or traffic patterns. However, after you spend a few weeks in the city, you develop your social and geographical comfort zones. You have *increased* your number of geographical comfort zones—not *exchanged* one for one. Comfort zones are not mutually exclusive; you can acquire as many as you like.

How a Comfort Zone May Help

Sometimes we find that a routine pattern of approaching things actually helps us get desired results. Preparing for the day, playing a sport, or organizing the annual meeting may have a pre-packaged approach that has proven itself to be a successful blueprint.

For example, to again quote from Dr. James Loehr, he noticed consistent patterns of behavior in tennis pros that allowed them to perform more regularly in their IPS—ideal performance state. Approaching the game the same way put the players in the right groove for top performance.

He writes: "I discovered a remarkable similarity among top competitors in the sequences of their thoughts and actions between points. The same movements, gestures, habits and rituals kept reappearing. Outwardly, it seemed as if they had all been trained in the same way and were following the same system." He then contrasts the people who followed patterns with those who apparently had no specific regimen: "In contrast, poor competitors were less disciplined, less exact, less ritualistic, and more varied in their actions between points." They had no obvious "groove."

I have observed the same behavior in how people go about any day during the week. I remember talking with a manager at a company who was very well read and seemed to have all of his ducks in a row. When I asked how he found time to read his five magazines each week and the newspaper every day, his response didn't surprise me:

"Every day, like clockwork, I come in to the office early and have some breakfast. I plan my day and read articles of interest in the newspaper and a couple of magazines. I may clip out articles I want to send to others or make notes in the margin for articles I will need to refer to later. I organize some items on my desk, and leave voice-mail messages early so people will have plenty of time to receive and respond to them. When I start my day with that quiet hour before the barrage of interruptions, I feel well informed and on track."

The important concept here is that a comfort zone should be the by-product of a bigger objective. It should be a routine that is constructive, not inhibitive and limiting; and and you should remain flexible enough that if you discovered a better alternative, you would be willing to make the modifications.

Mixed Feelings

We were born with conflicting desires. On one hand, as mentioned, we like to be safe, secure, familiar, stress-free, status-quo type of people. On the other hand, we like variety, new experiences, adventures, personal growth and enlightenment. We can't have it both ways. The latter requires us to break free from the former.

If we want circumstances in life to change, but follow the same routines, we'll become frustrated. That is like hoping the cake comes out of the oven tasting differently, but each time we put the same ingredients in the cake mix. You cannot expect a different outcome if the preparatory process remains the same.

I talk to people every day who, on the one hand, would like to take an evening class at a local university, but, on the other hand, have their Monday night football, Tuesday relaxation, Wednesday and Thursday favorite television shows, Friday social calendar, Saturday's errands, Sunday's read-the-paper/watch-sports/prepare-for-the-following-week routine. Somethin's gotta give!

Just like the cake-mix analogy, our activities are ingredients, and we will reap what we sow. If taking classes goes into the mix, then a degree, sooner or later will come out of it. If piano lessons go into the mix, then soon a piano player will emerge from the room. If taking the class is truly the objective, then forgoing television may be a small price to pay. There will be a cause-and-effect relationship between actions and results: We must take certain actions to create certain results.

To the degree that we can change inhibitive routines and comfort zones, we will experience more variety, more opportunity, and tap more of our potential—potential which may be limited only by our scope and experiences in the world. We must somehow liberate ourselves from past perceptions and routines in order to move in a direction more in line with what we feel is most important in life. The moment you hear yourself making excuses or backing out of a new opportunity simply because it is unfamiliar, tell yourself that you *must* walk in that direction.

Dr. M. Scott Peck, in his best-selling book *The Road Less Traveled*, emphasizes the importance of growth and change: ". . . no matter how seemingly healthy and spiritually evolved we are, there is still a part of us, however small, that does not want us to exert ourselves, that clings to the old and familiar, fearful of any change or effort, desiring comfort at any cost and absence of pain at any price, even if the penalty be ineffectiveness, stagnation or regression." If we keep moving and growing, we will never stagnate.

> All things must change
> to something new
> to something strange.
> HENRY WADSWORTH
> LONGFELLOW

Why Stay?

Although people understand the benefits of leaving a comfort zone, two fears keep them inside—the fear of failure and the fear of success.

Fear of Failure

If we never write the goal, then we're not obligated to pursue it; and if we're not obligated to pursue it, we don't run the risk of failing and letting ourselves down or giving other people

> Better to wear out than to
> rust out.
> BISHOP CUMBERLAND

any material for ribbing us. We can't be called any names if we don't make any mistakes. However, we can't win a race if we never enter the competition, and there's no glory in having zero losses and zero victories.

Most of the winners we know today became winners by learning from many previous failures. For example:

- A studio executive once dismissed Fred Astaire with the opinion "can't act . . . can't sing . . . balding . . . can dance a little."
- Charles Goodyear had so many business failures he was sent to debtor's prison. Later he accidentally discovered the vulcanization process that revolutionized the rubber industry.
- Abraham Lincoln began the Blackhawk War as a captain, but by the end of the war had been demoted to a private.

Your past does not determine your future. A past failure does not guarantee a future failure. You can avoid failure by concentrating on succeeding, thus creating better chances of getting what you want. Take a few chances, understand what needs to be done, remember that an occasional setback is to be expected, and the number of setbacks you experience has absolutely no bearing on your likelihood of succeeding—and it may even mean you are getting closer to a victory.

If you believe in the law of averages, failures are a step closer to a success. If you knock on ten doors selling newspaper subscriptions, and one person buys, you could assume that about ten percent of your prospects will buy. The next batch of ten doors you knock on could hold five consecutive "no's"—statistically, one in the final five knocks will bring success.

Fear of Success

There are those that are more comfortable when they are not the center of attention. If they don't climb the corporate ladder too quickly, then nobody will notice. If they did get a double promotion, the concern could be how their coworkers will react (jealousy, envy, ostracism). There are sometimes changes that accompany success: status quos, social circles, and increased responsibility. Our minds start racing at the the thought of what the price will be for actually getting what we want.

I taught a time management seminar at a brokerage firm in New York City, and the subject of comfort zones was raised. After it was discussed, we had a short break. The manager of the branch approached me and mentioned that he had a good story about a fear of success.

There was a broker in the office who had reached retirement age and would soon be turning his active client list back over to the firm. The existing client list this broker had developed was generating about $300,000 a year in commissions. The manager of the branch had to decide how the client list would be divided and determine who had the ability to successfully manage a demanding list of clients and busy schedule.

He said, "You would think that a broker who is in the business to provide service and earn money would jump at the chance to get a piece of the action. But after I made the presentation to some of the brokers individually, a few of them weren't so sure they wanted the extra business. They wanted to know if that meant they'd have to start work earlier or work later; they wanted to know if they would be expected to go out to more lunches or give more presentations on new products; they were wondering about having to change offices (within the same building), and if they would have more or less accountability to local management." Meanwhile my mind raced as to how fast I could update my résumé.

These are good questions to ask. But the manager of the firm made it clear to me that it was the way in which they asked the questions that gave him the impression that the brokers felt as if they had everything "just right" in the office; they feared that a new opportunity would change too many comfort zones. Some had concerns that other brokers would resent the fact that they got the new business and about how they would deal with the temporary shift in a social comfort zone. Although all admit to money as a motivator, they still tread cautiously.

Changing routines can be an important consideration. If you have a family, a spouse, or other people whose needs should be considered, then move more cautiously. But when hesitation is analyzed in a variety of situations, it usually is rooted in something trivial, something psychological, and something that can easily and painlessly be replaced by the new comfort zone.

Change is inevitable. You can try to fight it, if you'd like, but you'll find that things today are different than they were yesterday. This generation is very different from the previous. You should welcome change because it brings with it new challenges and new opportunities. The human being is an extremely resilient entity, and you somehow manage to adapt to changing economies, changing temperatures, and changing lifestyles without too much confusion. Rather than be forced to change when you *have* to, why not proactively change because you *want* to?

As you address your goals, be prepared to change some routines for a while, and change them with confidence, knowing that it is for all of the right reasons, and you'll be a better person for having made the changes.

Tapping potential will require changes in your daily routine and your daily schedule.

Action Items

- Consciously decide to do something different or change a routine if you feel it will make you a better person.
- Create a comfort zone or routine that will help you get better results (e.g. reading the newspaper every morning at 6 A.M.).
- Commit to doing something that will require you to push yourself a bit and rise to a new level of performance.

A DATE WITH POTENTIAL

There is no chance, no destiny, no fate, which
can circumvent, nor hinder, nor control, the firm
resolve of a determined soul.

ELLA WHEELER WILCOX

As I have mentioned several times there are many ingredients in the success and achievement formula, and it is a special, unique combination of these ingredients that will work for you.

The following four elements enable you to fully develop and utilize all of the ingredients I have discussed previously. These will act as the sunshine on your flower beds of potential that will put the principles into action. DATE is the acronym for these elements: Desire, Accountability, Time frame, and Energy.

Desire

You must really, really want to tap your potential. It must be a burning desire, otherwise the first snag will seem like a roadblock; the first failure will feel like a crushing defeat, and the first rejection will sound like a bankruptcy death knell. If you have ever been in a situation when you don't just want something, but you have an intense desire for it and actually crave it, you will know what I am talking about and understand the difference.

We have heard the stories about people who moved to New York or Hollywood to study acting and simply had to find work in order to survive. The now successful actors look back and laugh at their living conditions and what they had to do in order to

> If little labour,
>   little are our gaines:
> Man's fortunes are
>   according to his paines.
>   ROBERT HERRICK

eat. They remember having to lose weight, grow their hair, travel, knock on hundreds of doors, deal with rejection, find a way to "drop in" on someone important just to leave a script or a photograph. The need was present, the desire was intense, and so they persevered.

In Billy Wilder's classic film *Sunset Boulevard*, the main character, played by William Holden, needs to borrow some money in order to live while trying to write a script. The prospective wealthy loaner tells him "no" and reminds him that "some of the best material is written on an empty stomach." If failure becomes life threatening, we are willing to do whatever it takes to succeed.

I have mentioned earlier that the idea of dabbling in self improvement brings no results. Dabbling in anything rarely does; whether it is fitness, learning about computers, or investing in the stock market, there is a big difference in the results you get when you make something your passion versus when you just tinker with it. Sometimes what we think is our current "passion" may just be a temporary "kick." And when the kick loses its appeal, the desire disappears and we start something else. Make the pursuit of your goals your passion and see what a difference it can make.

We must realize as we pursue our goals that, as Heraclitus, the Greek philosopher, said, "A man is most nearly himself when he achieves the seriousness of a child at play."

I must admit, at times after a hard day at work, the thought of buckling down at the computer sounded dreadful. Dinner and anything relaxing and non-cerebral was all I was prepared for. But my *desire* to finish my book was so great and so important to me that if I managed to flip on the computer and start punching the keyboard, I would find myself gradually drawn into my work.

If I had an "information slide" (like a landslide only better and without the clean up) considerable time would pass and it would be almost midnight before I realized that I was "supposed to be tired." It reminds me of what Mark Twain said about our work: "Make a vacation out of your vocation and you'll never work a day in your life."

> There are two tragedies in life. One is not to get your heart's desire. The other is to get it.
> GEORGE BERNARD SHAW

Tapping your potential is a lifestyle and not a thirty-day trial program.

If you review your values and set your goals (remember the MOST formula?) you should discover things worth fighting for. You will uncover values that are not only important, but ones that serve as core motivators that inspire you to set goals. Sometimes people become distracted by what they see *now*, and it takes time away from what they want *most*. If you remember my puzzle from the chapter on goal setting, our core motivators must be our primary concern—the center of the puzzle.

This is not to suggest that if you wanted to be the finest golfer in the world that picking up the game of volleyball for a summer would have disastrous consequences. I'm referring to circumstances where people aren't sure of what they want and so they bounce from one idea to the next all of their lives and in the end are not truly gratified nor have much to show for their efforts.

Tapping your potential requires a strong desire to fully develop a particular aspect of your life.

Accountability

It may not be enough to leave tapping your potential to the powers of your own discipline. This may contradict much of what I

have been saying and what other
authors say about the powers of determination, but there is another ingredi-
ent you can add to making it happen.
It's called *accountability*.

> Pay every debt as if God
> wrote the bill.
> RALPH WALDO EMERSON

If you promised a friend to help them with their computer
software so they could use it to meet a deadline, you would follow through immediately. If you had planned to learn more
about your own computer software at some time, it could drift
for weeks. But because someone else needs you, and you feel
accountable to them, you take action. You can do the same thing
for yourself on a regular basis by *creating* accountability with others for the accomplishment of your goals.

Find people that are valuable resources to you in the accomplishment of your goals and make some commitments and
appointments. Set dates and times to meet with people to gather
and share information. Be willing to spend some money in the
pursuit of your goals. It doesn't have to be thousands of dollars in
travel or consulting fees, try buying someone lunch so you can
pick their brain. You'll be amazed at how focused you become
on your material and how you become determined to make
those lunches and dollars count for something. Not to mention
the fact that in the course of future conversations with people,
you may be asked how the work with your project is coming
along. Because you prefer to have a good answer, an intelligent
answer, you will make progress in order to protect the ego. Sure,
it is a little added pressure in your life, but it can serve as the very
impetus you need to get yourself moving in that direction.

I'll never forget the time I sat with my book consultant, Bob
Tinnon, on this project. He asked me a simple question that is
responsible for me starting and finishing this project:

"Ken, could you send me a couple of sample chapters in two
weeks?"

I had been thinking about writing a book for a long time.
Now I was being asked to put at least two of the chapters (about
15 percent) of the book in the mail in two weeks! I responded

with "Sure, no problem, Bob, would the week of the twentieth be okay?" And as I hung up the phone, I realized that there was now another human being relying on my ability to produce. My goals are most important to *me*, but apparently, that wasn't enough. When the project became important to *somebody else*, then I scrambled to make the effort. I wrote in the evenings, on airplanes, and researched on the weekends. If it wasn't for someone else's involvement, I was accountable to nobody else but me, and I'm pretty forgiving when it comes to procrastination. So I found someone else to push me a bit.

The cycle in tapping your potential is shortened when you are accountable to others.

I remember a few years ago a friend handed me a script he planned to submit to an agency. He needed to show it to a few people for their opinion and had to have my copy back the following day. He was hoping to get a thorough critique from me. In other words, not only did he want me to look at it, there was going to be a test at the end!

I would normally take three or four days for something like this and pace myself. But because of my need to return the script the next day, I got it done. I made the commitment to give my feedback, and now felt as if my agreement was more of a promise—a contract. What did I learn? *We are prompted into action whether the task is tied to our goals or somebody elses as long as the accountability is there.*

Time Frame

We established that although things may be highly valued in life, if the idea lacks urgency, or a calendared date, it will drift and quite possibly never happen. We prevent lost opportunities by creating time frames within which we plan to accomplish our tasks.

For example, there is a management principle called *Parkinson's Law*, that states "work expands so as to fill the time available for its completion." If you had two hours to tackle a one-hour project, it is likely to blossom—

> But at my back I always hear Time's winged chariot hurrying near.
> CHRISTOPHER MARLOWE

or expand, like an accordion—to fill the entire two hours. I have practiced this many times as I find myself with an entire Saturday free to go to the grocery store. It takes all day to get there.

On the other hand, if you are pressured to get a two-hour project finished in forty-five minutes, especially if the need is great enough, you can work miracles. The task will shrink and scrunch down, like an accordion, in order to fit within the time-frame. I have practiced this many times when friends are in the neighborhood and invite themselves over with about five minutes notice. I can clean an entire house and wallpaper a bathroom in a few minutes if people are headed over to my place.

So what have we learned? When the the need is great enough, we perform miracles. And usually the need is applied from the outside, externally. If there is no great need, it is more likely to be procrastinated. So the solution for a "lack of external need" is to create your own needs and time-demands from within, internally, and get years of work accomplished in weeks. Try this approach and you'll tap more potential in shorter time.

Energy

Tapping potential requires involvement and action on your part. You must get out of the locker room and out on the playing field in order to get results. You have to push yourself out of bed in the morning regardless of the weather, the fatigue, or the snooze button. You must put in the extra hour in the evening no matter how little you feel like it, no matter how funny the television program, or how tempting the social affair. This drive is a product of your reserves of energy. Energy is the ability to take action by creating the necessary motivation and vigor needed to accomplish specific objectives. Your energy levels can be enhanced by good purpose, exercise, and diet.

Tapping potential is not a question of who's the better philosopher, or who has the most knowledge, it is a question of who can consistently make the effort and invest more energy in the endeavor. Your energy level will manifest itself through your tenacity, the hours you can put into your projects, and your attentiveness. It is your rocket fuel that will propel and carry you throughout your journey.

Peter Vidmar, a friend and associate of mine and Olympic gold medalist, told me what it was that helped him become a champion.

He said that focusing on winning was part of what helped him win, coupled with the energy to train every day. While perhaps others on the gymnastics team at UCLA would cut a workout short, or skip a day, Peter was in the gym, regardless of the external circumstances or his internal drive. He mustered up the energy enthusiasm any way he could. It takes energy and resolve to steadfastly walk to the gym (or anywhere else for that matter) when you don't want to go.

He told me that to a certain point, everyone on any kind of team competes at a certain level; but as the rules change, challenges become greater, and the demands increase, you'll get some fallout. Winners are those that stick to their plans and projects through the vicissitudes of challenge. Once they commit, their energy reflects their resolve.

Tapping your potential requires energy focused on doing what you know to be helpful in getting results.

Slippery Language

I like to call vague, non-committal language "slippery." When you preface a task with slippery language you are able to weasel out of things you said you'd do. You haven't committed to a particular *time*. This is a convenient way to get out of dinner parties,

avoid goal setting, dentist appointments, reading, fitness routines, and
anything else worthwhile that you
avoid due to fear or procrastination.
The following are examples of slippery language:

soon
someday
when I get a chance
when I feel like it
this next New Year
right after my birthday
when I get the money
when the weather gets better
when I'm not so busy
as soon as my calendar clears
once the kids graduate
when the economy gets better

> I propose to fight it out
> on this line if it takes all
> summer.
> ULYSSES S. GRANT

All of these words and expressions are slippery because they
release us from the pseudo-obligation we created.

Slippery language provides an escape hatch. It will always be
an opportunity without ever having to commit us to a specific
time for taking action. This language is the standard jargon in the
lazy person's vocabulary. The reason: It never commits, it puts
the blame of inaction on the part of an external source (it's not
our fault), and the phrases themselves can be used year after year.
Just imagine! Not only do we put things off forever, we actually
use timeless excuses that can be used forever!

Because:

soon and someday are always just ahead
we are always busy doing other things
we could always feel "better" and more in the mood
the New Year is always within the next twelve months
so is your birthday

people could always use a little cash
the weather could always get better
we'll always be busy with a full calendar
okay, so maybe the kids will graduate
the economy could always improve

We need to start when we identify the goal; if we wait for all the conditions to be perfect, we will never get started. If I waited for all of the lights to be green before I left the house for work, I'd be housebound. We must eliminate the slippery language in order to change the behavior and take action.

The choices are simple. Take any of the slippery phrases and replace it with one of two (or both) of the following:

a specific time on the clock
a specific date on a calendar
both

This settles the problem of procrastination and avoidance.

"Soon" turns into 3 P.M.
"Someday" turns into Wednesday
or both: Wednesday at 3 P.M.

Problem solved. Toss in another person for an appointment or just to meet for lunch, and you have added the previous element of accountability. Problem *really* solved.

The cycle in tapping your potential is shortened when you apply urgency to the endeavor.

Exercise

I am not an expert in nutrition and fitness, but I know enough about it through personal experience to make some sound recommendations. I can tell you that besides issues of self-esteem and health, a body that is well maintained will carry you further than one that is not. A healthy body and one that is exercised on a regular basis is less susceptible to injury, disease, heart failure, high cholesterol, and many of the other misfortunes that are not entirely random; some of our physical challenges are self-imposed.

A well-maintained body will be a better provider of energy.

When the body is a well-maintained machine, we require less sleep, we have more efficient digestion processes, and our bodies are freed from adrenaline and cortisol, which are released when we become stressed. It becomes a cleaner burning high-performance engine that used to be a klunker. If we keep in mind that we simply feel better about ourselves (better attitude and self-esteem) when we take care of our bodies, we find a few more reasons why thirty minutes a day of exercise is a reasonable thing to do considering the return on investment.

This is not a beauty contest! The important point is that high achievers must sometimes put in more hours and have the physical and mental wherewithal to handle a fast pace. If the body isn't healthy enough to carry them through these challenges, it will quit and fall asleep, go home, or even collapse. Take care of the only vehicle you have to carry you through life.

Purpose and Energy

Wind your calendar back a few years and think about waking up on your birthday when you were a child. Were you sluggish and phlegmatic? If the thought of opening presents and being the center of attention for an entire day was altogether unappealing, then you may not have been real enthusiastic.

But for most kids, as they prepare for bed on the eve of a birthday, pleasant thoughts of what the day will bring puts the child to bed with a sound, happy mind. The conscious mind is allowed to rest, but the sub-conscious mind is still thinking and sorting what it has to look forward to. When the child awakens, he or she will spring to their feet and enthusiastically start the day. The reason: they have something to look forward to and the energy is created to carry them through the day.

> For a man seldom thinks with more earnestness of anything than he does of his dinner.
>
> SAMUEL JOHNSON

This is very much tied to the chapter on Purpose. If we know *why* we are getting out of bed, or why we do some work on the weekends and into the evenings, we will create the energy needed to meet the demands. When we don't care, the body burns out. That is why we see people mope around the office during the week, but then buzz through the office taking care of business and putting a few things in order on Friday afternoon. The energy is actually being pointed toward leaving the office and starting the weekend! A way to create energy is to create a meaningful agenda and purpose.

It reminds me of what Norman Cousins said in his book *Anatomy of an Illness as Perceived by the Patient*: "a highly developed purpose and the will to live are among the prime raw materials of human existence." (Does this remind you of my travel schedule through the Northeast when I had the flu?).

Diet

Something you learn very quickly when you keep a heavy travel and speaking schedule is that you cannot eat your heart's desire at every meal. Something as seemingly harmless as a soft drink can make speaking comfortably a challenge, not to mention what spicy foods, foreign foods, or lots of food in a single sitting can do to you. Quite by chance I have learned about diet and proper eating habits because of my professional demands.

For anybody looking to have more energy, I will suggest the following: eat less, and eat better. What is the favorite past time for families after the huge Thanksgiving day meal? A nap. The digestive system is so overwhelmed by all of the food, that the body's energy becomes dedicated to digesting the food at the expense of the energy we could use to do other things. We find it easier to sit, then recline, then fall face down into a couch. That may be okay for Thanksgiving, but if that's the way you feel at the office, you may want to make some changes in eating habits.

The food you eat at night (how much food and how late you eat it) can also interfere with your energy levels first thing in the morning. Studies show that for many people, digestion can utilize more nerve energy than almost anything else. Good home cooking can take as much as eight to twelve hours to digest. If you eat until it hurts, your body is burdened a second time trying to process the meal. So as you try to sleep and let your system recharge, your body is actually busy at work trying to digest what is still in the stomach. You wake up robbed of some truly quality rest time.

Dr. Clive McCay at Cornell University, conducted an experiment with—you guessed it—laboratory rats. In the experiment, one group of rats were allowed all the food they wanted, another group had their intake cut in half and it *doubled* their life span. Gradually cut back on the amount of food you eat and see if it doesn't make a difference. This will require you to "rethink" your perception of what a regular lunch is. We live in a culture where everything is the "triple," the "big gulp," the "super macho," the "forty ounce," the "hungry man," and the "combo."

You don't need it, even if it is cost effective. If what you save now, you pay for later in other ways, is it really worth it?

It is wise to feed and exercise your body in a way that it is conducive to more energy and healthier day-to-day living.

Keeping your DATE in mind will give you the added edge to apply the principles described in this book. I also recommend reading more on the subject of personal improvement. My book isn't the first on the subject, nor will it be the last. In order for material like this to take hold, you must immerse yourself in it. It is, in fact, a lifestyle.

Tapping your potential will require energy; and everything from purpose to your diet will be a factor in having large reserves of energy upon which you can draw.

Action Items

- Fix your mind on something you really, really want.
- Call someone today to get them involved in some aspect of your goals—it will create the needed accountability.
- Identify the part of your diet you will modify that will give you more energy on a consistent basis.

TQP (Total Quality People)

Training is everything. The peach was once a bitter almond; cauliflower is nothing but cabbage with a college education.

MARK TWAIN

Total Quality Management is a philosophy introduced to the business world by W. Edwards Deming in the 1950s. TQM had perhaps the greatest impact on management practice this century, and has been the basis of many training programs in corporate America.

Dr. Deming's theory contends that the *quality* of work produced is very much a result of the quality of the *process* by which it is produced. Managers are encouraged to evaluate and assess their management process to determine if it is bringing them desired results. They may need to change *how* they are to improve *who* they are. We have the same opportunity to apply the TQM theory to our own lives.

Deming identifies fourteen points that managers can focus on to improve their process and get better results. Some of those points are:

- Clarifying a sense of purpose
- Adopting new philosophies
- Continuous improvement
- Initiating programs for education and improvement
- Initiating plans of action

We can implement these same steps in order to become *Total Quality People*. For example:

Clarifying a Sense of Purpose. We discussed this earlier in the book. Purpose creates focus in life and is even life sustaining. You must know what you want in life. You must know why you get out of bed each day. You must have an agenda and something to look forward to. I'd recommend putting to paper the values and motivators that are the basis for your purpose in life. Your purpose may be to provide for others, inform the world, or to guide and counsel others.

Adopting New Philosophies. This is important as you learn more about the world around you. Is there a better mousetrap? Are there better ways to approach life? Are there new ways to think and act that will get you what you want? It is good at times to take some "philosophical blinders" off and consider some new thinking. The more informed you are about different philosophies, the more options you have to improve. Sometimes thinking differently and trying a new approach to your day (a new time management process as an example) can make all the difference in the world.

Continuous Improvement is Essential. Continuous personal improvement is a process and not an event. You are constantly evolving, so make part of that evolution an academic learning experience. Learn a new computer program, take an art class for fun, read a book about your profession or industry. Deciding to continuously learn (proactively) means you will improve by choice and not on demand when you have to. To decide *not* to change is a decision to stagnate at the expense what could be a better life. To decide to learn and grow feeds the spirit and the intellect.

Education and Improvement. Initiating these programs keeps companies on the cutting edge. While some companies have limited training opportunities due to schedules and budget, you can learn as much as you like on your own. The power is in your hands to pursue the classes, attend the seminars, and read the books needed to grow intellectually. The more you know, the more you can use, and the farther you'll go. Set an agenda for taking a series of classes, or set a goal to finish a number of units per semester toward an advanced degree.

Initiating Plans of Action. Put the fourteen-point theory to work! You must develop your plan of action for becoming a Total Quality Person. Create measurable goals for self-improvement. Put specific objectives in your calendar and get started immediately. Putting these plans in writing is critical. When you see it scheduled, it increases the commitment to implement.

The concept of Total Quality People is vital to your personal success and directly contributes to Total Quality Management efforts. After all, the quality of an organization can only be as high as the quality of its people.

Big Picture

The key to overall corporate improvement is to evenly apply new skills and processes throughout the entire company, not just for a segment of it. If you want to impact the organization, everyone should be part of the training. There should be a balanced approach to making the organization better.

> The best reformers the world has ever seen are those who begin on themselves.
> GEORGE BERNARD SHAW

Similarly, the key to overall personal improvement is to learn new skills that relate to the many different aspects of your life. You can't focus only on the financial or the physical aspects of your life—there must be attention given to other areas as well, such as the social, spiritual, and intellectual. I actually met a person who said every year he takes the stress management seminar! What about improving other areas of behavior that might reduce some of the stress in his life? He could benefit by looking at the big picture and realizing that there are many ways to improve performance and reduce stress.

I was working with a company a few years ago customizing some training programs. When we discussed who would be attending these programs, they mentioned there would be a cut-off point in the company—only directors and above.

I was happy to be working with the upper management of the organization, but wondered what was wrong with "the directors and below." Although some of the curriculum may not apply to administrative duties, there were hundreds of managers, engineers, and others who played on the same team and worked on a daily basis in meetings together to finish projects. There was a conscious decision being made to improve only an *area* of the organization. They weren't considering the big picture. What a shame.

The key in tapping personal or organizational potential will be implementing a balanced approach to improvement.

I have seen this lopsided approach to improvement on more than one occasion, and each time I make my suggestions but eventually do what the client requests. I can't help but compare this spot training to patchwork on the organizational fabric. It's like taking your car to the dealership for a detailing and waxing but requesting that only the hood of the car get waxed this visit—perhaps next month you'll get the trunk waxed and buffed. Some of the car shines, and some of it doesn't. Some of the organization shines, and some doesn't. The company overlooks an important synergy that could be created by having *everyone* buy into the same philosophy.

On the individual level, people naturally gravitate toward activities where they show a degree of proficiency. The person who hits a 275-yard drive on the golf course loves to go the driving range and hit balls for an hour. If putting is their weakness, it's more of a chore to stand and struggle with putting for the same length of time. As a result, the disparity between driver and putter performance grows.

Sometimes people take the classes and read the books where they "know all the answers" and they aren't truly challenged to think differently. As a result, they know everything about project management, but very little about writing or presentation skills. You must push yourself outside of your intellectual comfort zone in order to evenly apply the TQP theory.

Internal Versus External

I meet people who refuse to take seminars but buy any new electronic pocket device that has all of the modern bells and whistles that make it fun to use. They upgrade software, buy the new and improved cellular phone; purchase the beeper that scrolls messages on a liquid crystal display screen. These may be good tools, but the individual still has not gone through any changes yet. Learning, coupled with better tools, is what will make a lasting change. We must make both internal and external improvements. Sometimes we need writing skills, in addition to the fancy word processor.

It reminds me of the time I was pitching a series of training programs to an electronics company. They politely declined. The reason: "There really isn't any money allocated for training; we've never done much training in the past; and it's bad timing."

When I asked about the bad timing, they mentioned that there were some major building renovations under way to improve their corporate image, attract more clients, increase business, and serve as a morale booster for the employees who had heavy schedules. In other words, the changes would be external. A fountain with two angels spitting at each other in the lobby was more important than new skills; freshly laid turf in front of the building was more important than good tools to work with inside the building; the comfort of the Persian rugs and cushy chairs in the lobby was more

> If a man empties his purse into his head, no one can take that away from him.
> BENJAMIN FRANKLIN

important than training the people who sit in the chairs upstairs everyday. They hope to bring about changes in productivity, which actually involves a change in the *process*—but focused only on the external and cosmetic. They wanted total engine performance, so they painted the car. A Total Quality Management driven organization would have solved the problem by looking at how individual behavior and processes could be modified to improve the company. If they focused on making Total Quality People, some of their organizational objectives could be reached.

I have met many people who want to earn more money, climb the corporate ladder, and "be more successful." But instead of focusing on *internal*, behavioral changes, they focused on *external*, cosmetic changes. The best changes involve a balance of both.

A Moving Target

"Nailing" the method of successful living is difficult because "successful living" is a moving target. Our constantly changing responsibilities, values, and technology make the ongoing learning process inextricably

> I am still learning.
> MICHELANGELO

part of tapping our potential. With computers, the Internet, mind mapping, new computer software, e-mail, and other modern knowledge and tools, the demand for an increase in knowledge and awareness is ever-present; in meeting the demands of learning more, we accomplish the objective of increasing our ability to compete. In the same way that changing technology makes some products virtually obsolete, if we live in a changing world and decide to not change with it, we can become people dinosaurs. (Would you hire someone in your organization who was unfamiliar with a computer?)

The Cutting Edge

Perhaps the philosophy and truism of the importance of tapping our potential will never change. It has been endorsed over the years and it will persist over time. Yet the method and the means through which we tap our potential may always be changing. Sometimes in order to change and improve, we must first learn a few things that require a commitment to doing our homework. We need to increase our understanding about the means through which we can tap our potential. The objective in golf may never change, but the quality, weight, and materials used to construct a golf club and golf shoes may always be changing.

Years ago it was the tablet that was used as a tool in learning and efficiency; then came the quill, then the pencil, the ballpoint pen, the personal computer, the lap-top, and palm-top, the stylus, etc. What will tomorrow bring us? What could we have done years ago if we had developed some of the tools we have today? How much more potential could have been tapped? What could Socrates have done with a computer and the necessary training? And what may you be setting yourself up to forgo unless you continually learn and apply yourself?

> It is always in season for old men to learn.
>
> AESCHYLUS

Taking Full Advantage

I once sat next to a man on an airplane who asked what kind of business I was in. "Personal and organizational development," I told him. He asked me if that meant seminars. "Yes, that is part of what I do." He then said he went to something like that several years ago.

"I think it was in '82 I went to a two-hour time management thing, and back in '78 I went to a leadership gig."

I was saddened to hear that my livelihood and passions were affectionately referred to as "things" and

> When you are not practicing, remember, someone, somewhere is practicing . . . and when you meet them, they will win.
>
> SENATOR BILL BRADLEY

"gigs," but more surprised to see this man in his mid-forties felt those past experiences made him feel like he had all the bases covered today. He apparently wasn't seeking out any new information on the subject. (I see a dinosaur in seat 23C). But enough of him, let me finish with my gig.

When I asked if his company provided training, he told me "Yes, some project management and computer training, but I don't do that sort of thing. I've been with my company for a long time so I feel like I have my routine pretty well wired and I know what I am doing. Plus, sometimes you can't teach an old dog new tricks. Some of these seminars are great for college grads and entry-level types, but after twenty years in the business, if you haven't learned the ropes by now, you shouldn't be working for the company."

Does this sound like a Total Quality Person? He has made a conscious decision to avoid three very important points of the five points in TQP mentioned earlier; he's not interested in any new philosophies, not interested in improving personally, and avoids the seminars that are designed to help people at any stage in their lives or careers. Do words like stagnate, regress, and comfort zone come to mind? Continuously improving is an important element of the Total Quality theory—for businesses and people. What kind of potential is this person going to leave lying dormant? No one will ever know.

Tapping your potential involves taking full advantage of new knowledge and technology with the purpose of more fully developing your skills. You must continually improve in order to survive in a competitive world.

Household TQM

Take the case of the Sony Walkman, a world-class product, immensely popular, and very different than it was when first introduced. Look at its evolution:

Auto reverse
Bass and treble
Smaller headphones
Shock resistant
Waterproof
Electronic tuning
Smaller
Rechargeable batteries
Smaller again
Dolby
An alarm clock

And it will continue to change. To meet the changing demands of the consumers, the product must be refined and upgraded in order to compete. You and I live in a highly competitive world and need to meet the same criteria.

On Your Mark . . .

The by product of successfully applying the TQM philosophy is great products for the consumers. The rivalry between the airlines, soft-drink companies, computer companies, and car manufacturers means that products are always being fine-tuned and improved. There is an expressed form of competition among organizations that drives them to do things better for the consumer for fear that we'll walk away and they will file for bankruptcy. If we don't recognize that we live and operate in a similarly competitive world, we could suffer a talent bankruptcy.

High school seniors face the challenge of gaining acceptance to a college or university. Those with extracurricular activities on their résumé may have an advantage. Students who have traveled, learned to play an instrument, or who speak a different language may have a competitive advantage over others seeking the same limited number of seats in college. It is therefore important for students to improve, pursue, and develop new and unique talents.

> A man's mind may be likened to a garden, which may be intelligently cultivated or allowed to run wild; but whether cultivated or neglected, it must, and will, bring forth. If no useful seeds are put into it, then an abundance of useless weed seeds will fall therein, and continue to produce their kind.
>
> JAMES ALLEN

In business, we must work and compete against those who are better read, have better time-management and organizational skills, or who know how to manage an organization. Our associates may be speed readers, excellent public speakers, or be more computer literate than we are. Employment opportunities are based on past experiences and present knowledge. We are evaluated on who we are, and what we promise to be. It seems that no matter what we want in life, there are many people behind us, jockeying for the same position that establishes, again, the urgency to acquire more skills and knowledge.

In our world markets, some countries have a labor advantage, electronics advancements, or economic systems that are more efficient. It is this kind of environment that keeps students, employees, and companies around the world on their respective toes. Everyone is always looking over his or her shoulder and moving fast. If we work every day with a typewriter, we will soon become obsolete in a world of computer-literate people.

Whether you refer to it as Total Quality People or becoming a "sponge" for new information, it is a necessary process. A sad misconception is that after schooling, at any level, you are fully prepared to meet the world and its demands. You always need to continue to learn either through a formal school session or through self-study. You have the ability to acquire the skills, and you have skills and potential that have not been applied. You have potential that must be discovered and applied and enough innate talents to go out and acquire what you need.

The purpose of tapping your potential is to improve your life and put you in a position to have more choices and chances for opportunity.

It Goes Without Saying

I have yet to read a doctrine or philosophy opposed to the improvement of the mind. Call it what you will—intellectual exercise, mind aerobics, a cerebral workout—all of it is good for the soul and benefits the individual, sometimes directly, and sometimes in ways difficult to measure. But there does exist a cause-and-effect relationship between how you think and how you behave. James Allen, in his great work *As a Man Thinketh*, recommends placing only the most constructive seeds in our minds to bring forth desirable circumstances.

After having studied success over the years, I have found that people who do well not only know their jobs and areas of expertise, they believe that new knowledge, new skills, and an overall awareness of what is going on in the world around them is practical and will pay off in ways never expected.

It seems that education, not just focused expertise, is what is valuable in the long run because you will never know when an opportunity will present itself or when different demands will arise that will call upon your aptitudes in different areas. It is important that you proactively set an agenda for learning and improvement rather than trying to "learn on demand" as circumstances change.

You would be amazed to see how limited some people's "improvement philosophies" actually are. People openly admit that they never listen to educational tapes (on any subject), read maybe five or six books a year (for fun), and only attend a seminar if it is offered by their organization. Everybody agrees and understands that any one of these learning resources is valuable, yet only a percentage actually do something about it. Perhaps that is why there is only a small percentage of people who are the *best* at something.

Tapping your potential requires reading materials that increase your awareness and appreciation for the world around you.

Action Items

- Identify one skill you could acquire that would fortify your résumé or help you every day.
- Identify one of your present skills that could be refined or enhanced.
- Attend one seminar or read one book that will add to your pursuit of continuous personal improvement.

EPILOGUE

If a man has a talent and cannot use it,
he has failed. If he has a talent and uses
only half of it, he has partly failed.

If he has a talent and learns somehow
to use the whole of it, he has gloriously
succeeded, and won a satisfaction and
a triumph few men ever know.

THOMAS WOLFE

And so we arrive at the final page. You have been patient and
taken the time to read through the ideas and philosophies
involved in becoming all that you can for your good and for the
good of others. There is a lot to consider, no question about it.
But remember Confucius when he said "A journey of 10,000
miles begins with a single step"; I hope that these ideas are practical enough for you to begin your journey right away.

Writing a book is a long journey, and my finishing this book is
actual proof that "water does eventually wear away at the stone."
If you stick to your guns long enough, anything can be yours. I
felt compelled to write this book for one very simple reason: The
message is one of great importance. I have a sincere faith in people's ability to *do* what they want so they can *have* what they
want, and I feel this book will add to the quality of that endeavor
and could even make it possible.

In seminars over the years I have met many people who struggle a bit with life, professional obstacles, and personal challenges,

and that tells me something: People are always consciously or subconsciously involved in trying to add value to their lives. I have had many opportunities to encourage people to consider some solutions and possibilities that will add more value to their lives. This book provides another perspective and "spin" on the philosophy of human development.

Although we may not have met in person, we have been introduced here, through these words. It was nice meeting you. I hope that our time together will prove itself to be of lasting value to you, and that other books in the industry will also continue to serve you well.

I wish you the best of luck in all of your future endeavors.

REFERENCES

ALLEN, JAMES. *As a Man Thinketh*. New York: Grosset & Dunlap, n. d.

BLANCHARD, KENNETH, *The One-Minute Manager*. New York: William Morrow and Co., 1982

BASS, DICK. *Seven Summits*. New York: Warner Books, 1986

BLISS, EDWIN C. *Getting Things Done: The ABC's of Time Management*. New York: Scribner, 1991.

BRANDEN, NATHANIEL. *The Power of Self-Esteem*. Fla. Health Communications, Inc., 1992.

BARKER, JOEL ARTHUR. *Paradigms*, New York: HarperCollins, 1993

CARROLL, LEWIS. *Alice's Adventures in Wonderland*. New York: Bantam Books, 1981.

COUSINS, NORMAN. *The Healing Heart*. Toronto: George J. McLeod, 1983.

COVEY, STEPHEN, R. *The Seven Habits of Highly Effective People*. New York: Simon & Schuster, 1989.

———. *Principle-Centered Leadership*. New York: Simon and Schuster, 1990.

DEMING, W. EDWARDS. *Out of the Crisis*. Cambridge. Massachusetts Institute of Technology, Center for Advanced Engineering Study. 1944

ELIOT, ROBERT S, AND DENNIS L. BREO. *Is It Worth Dying for?* New York: Bantam, 1989.

FRANKL, VIKTOR E. *Man's Search for Meaning*. New York: Pocket Books, 1985.

HELMSTETTER, SHAD. *What to Say When You Talk to Yourself*. Scottsdale, Ariz. Grindle Press, 1987.

KUSHNER, HAROLD S. *When All You've Ever Wanted Isn't Enough*. New York: Summit Books, 1986.

LAKEIN, ALAN. *How to Get Control of Your Time and Your Life.* New York: Peter H. Wyden, Inc., 1974.

LOEHR, JAMES E. *Toughness Training for Life.* New York: Penguin Books, 1993.

NEWMAN, JAMES W. *Release Your Brakes!* New York: Warner Books, 1977.

PEALE, NORMAN VINCENT. *You Can if You Think You Can.* New York: Prentice Hall, 1974.

PECK, M. SCOTT. *The Road Less Traveled.* New York: Simon & Schuster, 1978.

SCHULLER, ROBERT H. *Tough Times Never Last, But Tough People Do!* Nashville. Thomas Nelson, Inc., 1983.

SINETAR, MARSHA. *Do What You Love; The Money Will Follow.* New York: Paulist Press, 1986.

SMITH, HYRUM W. *The 10 Natural Laws of Successful Time and Life Management.* New York: Warner Books, Inc., 1993.

WAITLEY, DENIS. *Seeds of Greatness.* New York: Pocket Books, 1983.

———. *Timing Is Everything.* Nashville. Thomas Nelson: Publishers, 1992.

———. *The New Dynamics of Winning.* New York: William Morrow and Co.